*Eyeballing
Big Croc*

Eyeballing Big Croc

Chasing Dreams Around The World

Vivien Zielin

Breezeway Books

Front cover inspired by a teapot
designed by Andy Titcomb Ceramics.

Some names have been changed
to protect the privacy of certain individuals.

© 2018 Vivien Zielin

All rights reserved. No part of this publication may be reproduced or transmitted in any form or by any means electronic or mechanical, including photocopy, recording, or any information storage and retrieval system, without permission in writing from the copyright owner.

Requests for permission to make copies of any part of this work should be mailed to Permissions Department, Breezeway Books, 7970 NW 4th Place, Plantation, FL 33324.

ISBN: 978-1-62550-542-2 PB
      978-1-62550-551-4 EB

Library of Congress Control Number: 2018907973

Contents

India
Eyeballing Big Croc	1
The Lotus Ponds of Lake Palace	4
How Does it Feel to be Related to a Statue?	8
A Very Special Meal	12
A Journey to Aurangabad	14

Nepal
Snubbing the Third Prince of Nepal	21

Kashmir
Elegant Ladies of Dal Lake	27
Pony Trekking in the Himalayas	31

Iran
A Day in Tehran	37

Israel
Six Days in June	43
Sing a Song of Soldiers	48
Fragments	49
Eilat	51
The Soldier From The Kibbutz	53
Skype Me	56
Do You Remember Esther?	59
Dressing Up	62

United Kingdom

Fearlessly Facing Little Croc	67
A Kaleidoscope of Colors.	70
A Million Miles from Hollywood	75
My Five Minutes of Fame	79
The Lecture	83
The Queen's Visit	86
Ballad of an Apple	89
The Man with a Table Leg	93
The Chicken or The Blouse?	97
A Star of a Street	102
The China Ware House Company	107
Three Tattooed Giants	115

The World

Around the World in a Hundred and One Days	123

Japan

A Passover Seder in Japan	129
A Thousand Fluttering Blossoms	133

Thailand

Monsoons and Showers	139

Bali, Indonesia

Tarantulas, Coconuts and Tropical Sunsets	147

The Trilogy-Russia and Ukraine-United Kingdom-Belarus

A Morning in Kiev with the KGB	153
A Hug Encircling The World	162
A Torah Returns Home to Baranovichi in Belarus	170

Canada

Bird Nests in the Skyhawk	183

British Virgin Islands
The Chief Minister is in The Shower   191

Costa Rica
Whitewater Rafting May 2011   199

St. Lucia and St. Kitts
Volcanoes, Trains, and Ocean Liners   203

United States of America
Almost Worth Breaking an Arm For   211
Michelin Boy   216
Are You Ready For The Next Adventure?   220
Chicken Soup, Poppadoms and Succotash   223
Pink Nails   227
Real Citizens   230

Acknowledgments   233

Eyeballing Big Croc

It was personal, definitely personal, no way was it imagination, the crocodile was grinning at me, its sword-edged jagged teeth glinting in the bright sunlight. He was a giant, by far the largest crocodile in the lake and was gliding across its surface, his long green snout resting on the shimmering water. He had perused the lakeside menu and was obviously contemplating the promise of perhaps a tasty English leg for hors d'oeuvres, followed by a more substantial British entrée...me. I had been sized up for lunch and found acceptable.

It was Thursday April 17, 1969 and we had arrived in Baroda in the state of Gujarat in India the previous day and had been welcomed by Vanita's family with a spicy and mouth-watering meal served on silver thalis. Chapatis, puris and poppadoms piled high, dahls and a medley of vegetables, rice, yoghurt with mint, lassi and finishing off with that queen of fruits: gorgeously flavorful golden juicy Alphonso mangoes. It had been a blazing hot day and the evening was humid.

"Let's sleep on the roof," suggested Vanita.

"Good idea," said her aunt.

Within thirty minutes, eight wood and string framed beds and white cotton sheets appeared as if by magic on the flat roof and we all fell asleep under a canopy of stars lulled by a symphony of croaking frogs, humming electricity and the lilting sounds of a distant sitar.

But what you may well ask has that to do with me eyeballing a crocodile? Well on my arrival in Baroda the previous day, I had been childishly delighted by a glimpse of wild monkeys swinging from tree to tree down Baroda's main street completely ignoring the flurry of traffic and people below. This proof that wildlife existed outside cages had produced a demand for something a little more dangerous.

"I've just the thing for you," Vanita had responded, "the Maharaja of Baroda's crocodile farm. It's located in the gardens of his palace; he breeds them and sells them to zoos all over the world. I hope that fits with your concept of wild."

"That will do for a start," I had replied.

So here we were, gradually moving closer to a bridge that crossed one section of the lake in order to get a better view of the crocodiles at feeding time.

Suddenly, a keeper appeared from a small hut beside the lake sporting half a left arm. It was missing from the elbow down and the fleshy stump wobbled as he walked. He let out a strange call and picked up a flag of bloody looking meat holding it high. He seemed to be summoning them. Sinisterly, three crocodiles came sliding onto the bank of the lake, including my saw-toothed grinning friend.

Whereupon, the keeper, with a total disregard for the safety of his other arm, started slapping them across their snouts with the flag of meat in an effort to persuade them to open their powerful jaws for the benefit of us visitors. It worked. Open they did with "Big Croc" easily the winner clamping his jaws tight around the prize, blood oozing around his teeth. He turned quickly, threshing his powerful tail, and with what appeared to be *a you next look* slid back into the lake.

The keeper threw more chunks of meat into the lake and powerful jaws competed for the food.

The display was obviously for our benefit and after a while the keeper turned towards us and said,

"Magnificent creatures aren't they?"

"Yes," we chorused back.

Then, looking straight at me with more than a hint of challenge in his voice, he asked,

"Would you like to sit on one and have your photo taken?"

Sit on one! Did he think I was totally crazy? Perhaps he believed the saying about 'Mad dogs and Englishmen.' After all, we were out in the midday sun.

My mouth had fallen open in disbelief and for once I was lost for words.

"Yes," he continued grinning, "we had a lady here from Australia last month and she sat on that crocodile's back." He pointed to one of the smaller beasts.

"I took her picture and she sent me a copy. Look, here it is." He rubbed his hand dry on his trousers and pulled a crumpled photo from his back pocket and, yes, there was a beaming woman with staring eyes perched on a crocodile.

This was it: a major challenge, a war of reputations. Reckless, crazy Australian versus sensible wimpy Brit.

Was I going to let my country and the empire down?

The answer was clear and obvious, not a doubt in my mind. Of course I was. I was not going to play this Indian version of "chicken."

So regardless of national pride, I smiled a smile of amazement and threw out the line, "Well, we all know about crazy Australians," and beat a hasty retreat.

The keeper looked really disappointed, but I could swear I saw 'Big Croc" glint a quick wink and swish his tail in an "I'll get you next time" gesture.

Interestingly, I found that my appetite for more wild animals had suddenly disappeared.

The Lotus Ponds
of Lake Palace

James Bond eat your heart out. I was there first in April 1969, speeding across Lake Pichola in Udaipur in the state of Rajasthan on a motor launch to visit the magical kingdom of Lake Palace. Hollywood was to take a while to catch up with the film *Octopussy* many years later.

The sky was velvet black over the lake, lit by a full moon and sparklers of stars. On the distant shore, the city of Udaipur flickered and danced with hundreds and hundreds of lights, a fairyland masking the harsh reality of people's daily lives. The faint sound of fireflies crackled in the air backed by a chorus of chirping frogs. In the distance, the outline of the second palace on the lake, Jag Mandir Palace, was a silent shadow.

I was sitting tucked into one of the palace's turrets, the water of the lake gently lapping at my feet. A cool breeze was blowing. It felt so good after the scorching heat of the day. Behind me, the flowered gardens, lotus ponds and beautifully tiled courtyards with their splashing fountains sparkled in the bright moonlight. This white marble lotus filled former summer palace of the Rajasthan royal family was indeed the stuff of fantasies. I sat reflecting on the day's events.

With skillful fingers, Vanita had tucked the folds of the sari into my waistband and draped the silky fabric over my shoulder.

"Look how elegant you look."

It felt so strange. This was to be my first public attempt at wearing a sari, that beautiful turquoise piece of shimmering silk, purchased earlier in the day from Udaipur's bustling market. The artist palette selection of silks had been stunning: cool rivers of blues, greens, gold and silver gliding through my fingers. So difficult to make a choice.

"Take the turquoise," Vanita had said. "It brings out the color of your eyes."

Now we were waiting for the hotel's motor launch to take us to the house of Rajeev, a business contact of Vanita's family. A white coated red-turbaned boatman helped us aboard, and in my flowing attire I did indeed feel elegant.

A car and driver was waiting for us when we arrived ashore. Twenty minutes later, we were walking into the lantern-filled courtyard of a large white villa. The courtyard was crowded with women in brightly colored saris and men in white tunic style suits. Rajeev, a tall man with an imposing black moustache, welcomed us. Waiters glided past with food and drinks.

"What would you like to drink?" Rajeev asked, "Whisky I'm sure," he said looking at me. "You British love a good whisky. Lemonade for you?" he said to Vanita. It was more of an assumption than a question.

I looked at Vanita and grinned as we had discussed this before arriving. Vanita was the whisky drinker, but had explained that, as an Indian woman, it would not be offered to her. Me, I hardly ever touched the stuff, but it had been agreed I would make an exception this evening so as not to offend the host.

"Yes whisky and soda please." I replied.

Rajeev gave an imperious wave and said something to the closest waiter who disappeared for a few minutes to reappear with a pitcher of lemonade and a very tall cool looking glass full of a light amber liquid. Another waiter prepared a table for us to sit at close to a large fan. Some friends of Vanita's family came to join us and we chatted about our trip across country and my impressions of India.

I took a sip of the amber liquid from the cool glass. It tasted sweet and had a syrupy texture and was unlike any other whisky I had encountered. I actually liked it and was content to keep sipping it.

The evening passed in a mixture of chatter, spicy food and tabla and sitar playing. After an hour or so, a group of four bejeweled women in bright flowing blouses and trousers began a graceful dance in the center of the courtyard with stylized hand and foot movements.

"Well Vivien, what do you think of our beautiful traditional music and dance?" asked a genial voice as Rajeev towered over me. He spotted my empty glass and clicked his fingers for the waiter to bring me another. The evening meandered on. It was all very pleasant.

Suddenly, I noticed that the number of dancers had increased and there were now eight weaving figures swaying from side to side. The crowd of guests also seemed to have doubled and were moving and blurring to form abstract art color combinations. The fans were also whirling wildly and had doubled and tripled in numbers.

"Are you all right?" a distant and vaguely familiar voice asked.

Everything was at least double and blurred and I felt distinctly queasy. I was certainly not all right. An echoing voice boomed somewhere behind me.

"Your friend seems to be a bit pale, I'll call the car to take you back to Lake Palace." Rajeev smiled smugly and continued. "It's the food. These Westerners can never manage it."

"Nonsense," Vanita replied, "Vivien loves our spicy food and is used to eating it. It's not the food."

Realization suddenly dawned. "What did you give her to drink? What was in that glass?"

Rajeev hesitated for a moment and then smirked, "Well I wanted to give our guest a taste of the real India. It was Asha, a royal palace liquor."

"What!" Vanita exploded. "You gave her a beer glass size of

home-brewed palace liquor?"

"Yes," he laughed. "It broke my heart to give her such a lot of my precious vintage, but I had to be generous to our British guest. It won't do any real harm. She'll sleep it off."

He glided away obviously highly amused at making this visible representation of once hated British imperialism look mildly ridiculous.

"It's okay," I muttered. "It tasted really nice. No harm done."

Vanita grinned, "Well, I suppose you can count yourself privileged. Most people never get to taste Asha, the queen of the palace liquor."

Much later that night listening to the waves gently lapping against the turret, with the bright moon highlighting the mesmerizing beauty of the white marble Lake Palace with its lotus filled ponds and courtyard gardens, I felt the cool breeze gently brush away any hint of Asha's effects. What did a slight hangover matter? It was all a part of this wonderful tapestry of adventure that was my visit to India.

What's it Like Being Related to a Statue?

"What's it like being related to a statue?" I asked as the car raced around the statue situated in the middle of a New Delhi Street at rush hour.

"You know nobody has ever asked me that before," answered the son of Sardar Patel, India's first deputy Prime Minister. "It's just something I have never thought about."

It was all a trifle bizarre. Here was I, sitting in a car with Dahyabhai Patel, a leader of the opposition Swatantra Party and heading to a meeting with one of the statue's successors, Mararji Desai. It had all come about because Vanita's aunt had picked up the phone and called her good friend Morarji to say that if he had the time, he had to meet her niece and a friend visiting India from England. After this morning's events, I was not at all sure what was going to happen.

It was the morning of May 1, 1969. We had been told that the Prime Minister Indira Gandhi met the public on certain mornings at 9:00 a.m. in her residence gardens and that it had been arranged for us to attend one such public meeting. Thus 8:30 a.m. found us waiting to be scrutinized by the security guards at the gate of her official residence. Walking through the gates, we saw a crowd of people milling around, but no sign of the prime minister.

Suddenly, a secretary appeared with a clipboard in his hands. He looked down his list of names and called, "Vanita Patel and Vivien Zielin follow me."

We looked at each other in astonishment.

"What's going on?" I said. "The prime minister is meant to come out of the house, not us go in."

We followed the quickly moving secretary along the corridor.

"Wait here a moment," he said pointing to some chairs in an alcove at the end of the corridor. What was happening? Were we about to be arrested? We had been assured that it was okay for us to be here among the public.

The secretary knocked on a door and disappeared. He reappeared moments later and beckoned us to follow him into the room which we did with some trepidation. The door shut behind him softly and he was gone.

We were standing in a very small study lined with bookshelves and with just enough room for a large wooden desk and small sofa. Sitting behind the desk, was a rather tired looking Indira Gandhi. There was no one else in the room besides Vanita and myself.

I nearly fell over in amazement. How unexpected! Why were we here?

With our hands pressed together and smiling we both gave the traditional namaste greetings to the prime minister.

"Sit down, please" the prime minister said and then there was an awkward silence.

Vanita, never lost for words, started to introduce herself speaking briefly of her father, a Member of Parliament and founder of India's first tractor factory and of her postgraduate studies in England at Sussex University which she explained was where our friendship started. The prime minister made minimal comment.

Straining to nurture this very stilted conversation, Vanita said brightly, "Vivien has been teaching on a kibbutz and has come here directly from Israel."

That did it, for this was an absolute conversational killer for a prime minister noted for her lack of enthusiasm for anything to do with Israel. Absolute stony silence. A hidden bell summoned the harassed looking secretary who opened the door and ushered us back out into the corridor and then to the garden.

A moment later, we watched Indira Gandhi sweep out to greet the many more people who were now gathered in the garden. A few words here and there; some murmured complaints, smiles for a posed photograph and then the Prime Minister was whisked back to her busy schedule, the rest of us meandering out past the ever-watching guards.

"What was that all about?" I exclaimed, "What were we doing there in a private audience? She obviously had no interest in speaking to us. Indeed, why should she?"

The best explanation we came up with was that Vanita's family connection with the independence movement and politics had been noticed and so a brief audience had been deemed a courtesy.

Thus, following the morning's events, my feelings about this second meeting with a major political figure were, to put it mildly, a trifle negative. Morarji Desai after all, had a public image as a dour man of austerity, who had married his wife when he was fifteen and she was nine and believed in the health benefits of drinking your own urine. What could we possibly talk about? This was certainly going to be a strain of a meeting.

I could have not been more wrong. To my surprise, the evening was a delight with interesting banter and conversation, way different from the morning encounter.

Vanita's aunt ushered us into a comfortable homely room, where our genial host greeted us with a warm welcoming smile and offered us refreshments of a non-controversial nature: tea and refreshing lemonade. Morarji immediately began asking Vanita about her time at Sussex University and her impressions of England, and then, with a smile at Vanita's aunt and a twinkle in his eye, he began to ask her when she was going to get married.

"You know I have been married to my wife for many years. We met as children. Marriage is the best basis for a happy life."

Vanita, well experienced in efforts to encourage her matrimonial status, skillfully changed the subject moving on to her hopes to continue her graduate studies in America. Her aunt looked a trifle exasperated.

Moving on to a new subject, the deputy prime minister turned to me and asked,

"What are your impressions of India?"

"It's fascinating experiencing the reality rather than hearing about the stereotypes." I replied. "It all feels so wonderfully vibrant: the vivid colors, the spices and the friendly people I am meeting."

"What were you doing in Israel?" he continued.

I explained that I had been teaching English on a kibbutz in northern Israel near the Lebanese and old Syrian border and that I had been living in a house that had had to be rebuilt because it had been demolished by Syrian artillery located on an overlooking hill during the Six-Day War.

Then, in a moment of chutzpah that I just could not resist, I asked if I could ask him something.

He looked at me with a keen and wise expression on his face.

"Go ahead."

I drew a breath and asked India's deputy prime minister, "Would you explain India's relationship with Israel?"

He looked long and hard at me and replied, "I will answer your question if you promise to keep it 'off record' and not release it to the press."

I agreed and his answer was honest and direct and political dynamite for a man who was later to become Prime Minister.

However, tempting though it was to go public, I never did. I kept my word.

Years later, when he became Prime Minister and I read press releases about "this austere severe man," I remembered a warm friendly evening with a man with humor, honesty and a grandfatherly twinkle in his eye.

A Very Special Meal

I was keyed up with anticipation and more than a little flattered. After all, I had never before had a dish specially prepared in my honor for a social event.

It was early evening in New Delhi. We had been invited by friends of Vanita's family for dinner. Vanita and I had arrived from Bombay a few days earlier and were staying with her aunt and uncle at the start of our travels through India, Kashmir and Nepal.

It was proving to be a very enjoyable evening. I had been introduced to an array of relatives and friends and the conversation flowed easily as we chatted under spinning fans, sipping cooling glasses of iced lemon.

The long table at the center of the room was covered with a white tablecloth and garlands of flowers and presented a panorama of delight with a mouthwatering display of food. It was an artist's palette with an amazing range of colorful delicacies arranged on silver thalis and bowls. Steaming curries, Chana

Masala, Saaag Paneer, Aloo Matar, rice, dhal, chutneys and puris, chapatis and poppadoms. The heady aroma of exotic spices, coriander, cumin, saffron, cinnamon and ginger wafted through the sultry evening air like a whirling aphrodisiac. I couldn't wait to start what was obviously going to be a really tasty and flavorful meal.

As the conversation buzzed around me, I was mentally composing a brief thank you for the special dish that was about to appear. I would mention the mouthwatering delights of Indian cooking as compared to England's bland food, adding that my taste buds had been honed in a Jewish home with tastier traditional dishes.

My thoughts were interrupted as Anokhi, our hostess, elegant in a silk blue sari, appeared carrying a silver platter and a casserole. She placed the dish carefully on the table and said, "Welcome Vivien. We have prepared this traditional dish especially for you so you will feel truly at home here. We hope you will enjoy it. Come on everyone, let's eat."

My tongue started to tingle in anticipation and my taste buds started dancing for joy. What new flavorful delight was about to appear?

As a servant moved forward and lifted the casserole lid, suddenly everything changed. I struggled to keep smiling and to stop the disappointment and dismay from flashing across my face. Resting in the casserole in splendid isolation was a dish of boiled cabbage, unspiced and bland. Just a few specks of paprika rouged its otherwise colorless and unpalatable strands.

I stood there speechless. I had always disliked boiled cabbage. How was I going to praise, let alone force myself to eat this insipid dish, which had been prepared by my hostess with such care and generous hospitality? I struggled to find the true British spirit necessary to digest this traditional British dish. Believe me, it was not easy.

A Journey to Aurangabad

I fumbled nervously for my flashlight in the swelteringly hot room. I had been awakened by a noise and it wasn't the sound of the creaking ceiling fan ineffectively whirling the hot air. I sat there fearfully on the edge of the bed in my damp T-shirt as the shadows of the moonlit palm trees danced menacingly across the bare walls.

Was my imagination working overtime yet again or was there really something in my room?

As I gingerly felt for my flip-flops, yesterday's events flashed back into mind.

I had arrived in Aurangabad around midday on June 18, 1969, following an overnight bus ride from Bombay. Vanita had waved me aboard with last minute reminders about my hotel and which bus stop to get off.

"Are you sure that you are going to be alright on your own?" she asked as I claimed a seat with my backpack.

"Of course. You know how much I want to visit the Ellora and Ajanta caves. You have booked me a hotel and told me where to get off the bus. What can go wrong? Don't worry I'll be fine."

"Okay. If you are sure. I'll see you back in Bombay in three days time. Enjoy yourself."

With a loud blast of its horn, the bus started to move as last minute travelers jumped aboard. It was a full house with everyone trying to find some comfortable space as we moved slowly through the heavy traffic of the hot crowded streets. Gradually we picked up speed and left the city far behind. The humid evening air came rushing in through the open-curtained windows, wafting a mixture of dust and pungent spices. As the only European aboard, I was the object of some curiosity and much friendly hospitality and, throughout the journey, I was offered and enjoyed a medley of tasty and tongue tingling spicy snacks. At each bus stop, some reached their destinations, while others climbed aboard in a mixture of colorful saris and white dhotis. As night fell, the bus grew quiet as we twisted and turned trying to find a comfortable spot to sleep in the clammy heat.

The next day, the sun was blazing overhead as I climbed down the bus steps into Aurangabad's dusty square and I was immediately engulfed by a crowd of tricycle rickshaw drivers vying for my attention. I handed a card with the name and address of my hotel to the driver closest to me.

"Yes, yes. I can take you," he said and quoted a price that seemed reasonable. The other drivers disappeared to surround other passengers getting off the bus, as my driver took my backpack and helped me into the back of the rickshaw. I watched as he arched over the cycle handles and started to peddle, his muscles rippling as he navigated through dusty streets. The heat was overwhelming and the markets and open bazaars began to shimmy and dance as my eyelids started to close.

"Don't fall asleep," I kept telling myself. "You'll be arriving at the hotel in a few minutes."

I was jolted awake sometime later as the rickshaw bumped over a pothole. I felt totally disorientated. We seemed to be traveling on a dirt track out in open countryside with very few houses in sight and nothing looking remotely like a hotel. I looked at my watch and saw with some alarm that I had been traveling for some forty minutes. Vanita had told me the hotel was a ten-minute ride from the bus stop.

"Where's my hotel?" I yelled loudly at the back of my driver.

"Soon be there don't worry," he said looking at me quickly and turning the pedals even faster.

He looked normal enough, but my eyes kept focusing on endless dry parched fields and an ever-distant horizon shimmering in a heat haze.

Where was I being taken? Was I being kidnapped? Was I going to disappear mysteriously never to be seen again?

I felt myself growing tenser and tenser. What could I do?

I was being driven away from my destination by a complete stranger in an unfamiliar place with no one around. Perhaps different parts of me would be found scattered across the Indian countryside, a human jigsaw puzzle that Interpol would never be able to solve. My poor parents would be inconsolable. I should have listened to my mother and stayed at home.

My imagination was going into overdrive as waves of panic took over. How could I have let this happen? How was I going to get away and escape this developing nightmare? I slumped back under the hood of the rickshaw confused and frightened.

I was so caught up in this irrational scenario that I had failed to notice that the fields were turning into streets and bungalows with gardens. Suddenly the driver stopped in front of a white washed two story building in a flowered courtyard.

Turning round and completely unaware of the state of terror I had talked myself into just a few minutes before, he said, "Here we are. This is your hotel."

He was right. It was my hotel.

He took my backpack and helped me down as I sheepishly followed him into the cool reception area feeling like a complete idiot. I paid him the agreed rupees and he smiled and left.

I was feeling hot, tired and more than a little bit confused.

"Welcome. We have your reservation," the receptionist said as I handed him my passport.

"Excuse me," I asked. "I was told your hotel was just ten minutes from the bus station, but it's taken me nearly an hour to get here."

"Which bus station?" asked the receptionist. "There are two main stops in the town and we are the second. The first is some fifteen miles away."

The penny dropped. What an idiot. I had gotten off at the wrong stop, and the rickshaw driver must have circled out of town to get me here.

Watching my expression the receptionist laughed. "A lot of backpackers make that mistake. Here are your keys. Dinner will be served on the veranda at 6:00 p.m. and we have your Ellora and Ajanta tour arranged for 7:00 a.m. tomorrow. Enjoy your stay."

Those words came back to me as I fumbled for my flip-flops and again heard the strange noise that had disturbed my slumbers. It was a scratchy, squeaky, creepy sound. What was it? Flashing my torch, I stumbled towards the light switch and flipped it on. The menacing palm shadows dancing on the ceiling disappeared as the room was flooded with light, illuminating the pastel colored walls, bamboo furniture and vases of flowers. Not a sign of an intruder.

As I stood there looking around, I heard a squeaking noise followed by a pitter-patter. It was coming from the bathroom. I rushed in determined to confront the monster. Again, the light showed nothing. I looked around puzzled at the Victorian style bathtub and then the sink and burst out laughing. Mystery solved.

Parallel tracks of mouse prints were running across the surface of my bar of soap. Yet another false alarm. It was just some mice come out to frolic in the midnight moonlight. It was time to get some sleep and allow my hyperactive imagination some rest so I could actually focus on the reason for this trip: to enjoy the frescoes and carvings of the Ellora and Ajanta caves.

Snubbing
The Third Prince of Nepal

The room was smoky with a low buzz of conversation and waiters darting between the tables with all manner of cocktails. Small groups of people were clustered around the roulette and blackjack tables in what appeared to be a normal casino scene.

But this was no snobbish Monte Carlo with traditional reserve, nor garish Las Vegas with its constant stream of distraction, nor indeed was it a 1930's gangster style gambling boat off Macau with sinister looking characters betting with golf balls. This was something else.

It was the Soaltee Casino set high in the hills of Kathmandu. Here there was as much interesting action outside the casino as in it.

It was May 7, 1969, and earlier that day we had awoken before dawn to drive out of town to Nagarkot to see the sun rise over the Everest range. The Tibetan Refugee camp was quiet as were the tangle of streets with their occupants still asleep. Villages, terraced fields and the figures of heavily laden men taking their goods to market, flashed past as we raced to catch the rising sun. Then, suddenly, an amazing vista was before us. High above a range of hills, seemingly balanced above the clouds, was a panorama of snowy peaks, a necklace of diamonds glinting in the early morning rays. Mount Everest did not jump out as the highest peak, but somehow it did not matter. Steaming cups of tea and toast from the outpost café had never tasted so good.

Later that day as we drove back to Kathmandu, we found the way blocked by a procession. Jumping out of the car, we were greeted by about twenty villagers proudly parading through town following two long poles, each supported by four villagers. Strapped to the poles by their legs, their heads covered by bloody brown paper bags were two huge tigers. They had been terrorizing some outlying villages, attacking children and carrying off goats and other animals, so the men of the village had banded together and, armed with just sticks, had tracked and trapped the tigers and were now heading to the royal palace to claim the bounty King Mahendra paid for dangerous animals who threatened his citizens. The whole procession came to a stop and beamed as I recorded the scene for posterity.

Now following an active day, we were enjoying a relaxing evening in the Hotel Soaltee's Casino. I was here in Nepal because of a challenge by my friend Vanita at Sussex University to come to the India Subcontinent to look beyond the stereotypes and experience how it really was. Our host in Katmandu, Subhash (a friend of Vanita's family) was at the blackjack table and Vanita and I were watching the intricacies of play. Out of the corner of my eye, I suddenly saw a man in a white linen suit with a lined leathery face slide onto a chair at the end of the table.

"Who's that?" I asked Vanita.

"Haven't got a clue," she whispered back. "Look, Sebhash just won that hand."

"Would you ladies like a cigarette?" The deep voice was somewhere behind my right ear. I turned to see a well-manicured hand holding out an art deco style silver cigarette case.

"No, thank you. We don't smoke," I replied.

"Well, how about a drink? What would you both like?"

"No. Thank you very much," Vanita cut in more curtly.

We both moved closer to the players, hoping he would take the hint and go away.

"Are you sure?" the persistent man continued. "Your glasses look empty."

We looked at each other; this guy had a really thick skin. It was time for a clear and unequivocal brush off.

Just as we were about to speak, we became aware of a sudden silence, an unnerving stillness. Everything around the table had gone quiet, play had stopped. Looking up, I saw everyone around the blackjack table was standing up and Subhash was in the process of going into a deep bow. At the same time, sensing something undiplomatic had been about to happen, his voice rang out loud and clear. "Vanita and Vivien. May I have the privilege of introducing you to his Highness, The Third Prince of Nepal."

Biting back the sarcastic comments that had been on the tip of our tongues and trying not to laugh, we stood up and shook his hand.

Saved by a bow from insulting a royal prince. What an escape!

Under the circumstances, we decided to pursue the more diplomatic path and accept the gin and tonic on offer and make some polite conversation before retiring for the night.

In my diary of the day's events, inverted snob that I am, I enjoyed recording the words, "Snubbed The Third Prince of Nepal."

My observation was obviously spot on, as confirmed by a sequel the next day. Subhash was taking a stroll in the beautiful lush gardens of the Soaltee Hotel and bumped into the Third Prince who said, "Subhash, who were those women you were with last night in the casino?"

Subhash, ever the diplomat replied, "Oh your highness, I introduced you. Vanita from Bombay and Vivien from London. They are visiting for a few days before traveling onto Srinigar in Kashmir."

"Oh," said the prince. "I thought they were trying to snub me."

Elegant Ladies of Dal Lake

It was like a silent film set with a shaft of bright moonlight acting as a spotlight to pick out the names of those elegant ladies of Dal Lake in Srinagar, Kashmir. The names had a lyrical ring to them: *Princess of the Mountains, Golden River of Spring, Blossom of the Lake, and Vale of Kashmir* to name just a few.

They swayed majestically in the moonlight swell, these glorious houseboats as stately as grand country houses, with their paneled ensuite bedrooms, formal dining rooms, grand ornate lounges and veranda decks. A perfect location for traditional high tea and evening gin cocktails in the rapidly fading colonial style. The now silent small kitchen boats were anchored alongside and in a few hours they would be bustling with boiling pots and pans.

Now all was quiet with just the sound of waves splashing gently against the regal wooden hulls. However, at daybreak, when the rising sun touched the waters in wondrous rose hues, Dal Lake, fringed by snowy peaks and surrounded by Mughal gardens, would come alive with scores of colorful shikaras or water taxis. These picturesque Cleopatra-style boats, with tasseled canopies and deep cushioned seats would skim across the lake propelled by skillfully maneuvered heart-shaped paddles.

All day the lake would be alive with the color and movement of shikaras ferrying passengers to and fro, displaying their wares, flower, fruit and vegetable shikaras piled high and shikaras loaded with leather, suede hats, gloves and bags. The tailor, smilingly climbing aboard the houseboat with his pattern book of choice Kashmiri cloths, the jeweler displaying his hand worked silverware. The nutcrackers, skillfully carved bowls and ornaments that suddenly appeared at our feet on the veranda deck as if by magic.

These would be followed at more regular intervals by the more stately progress of official shikaras. The post office, with its small red mobile letterbox, and the red and blue uniformed police sergeant being ferried along by his two subordinates. The hustle and bustle continued till twilight when the flurry was illuminated by twinkling fairy lights.

We had flown here from Delhi two days earlier on May 15, 1969, and had been relaxing and enjoying the novelty of being at the center of Dal Lake's fascinating and ever changing everyday theater. Now fully refreshed, we were waiting impatiently to be ferried to the shore to explore Srinagar's hodgepodge of lanes and alleyways bursting with handicrafts.

Once ashore, we meandered for hours enjoying the medley of sights and spicy smells and later that afternoon were to be found standing knee deep in bags–gorgeous light tan colored leather bags-each one with an intricate embroidery design.

It had all started when I suddenly spotted a small store on one of the side streets chock-full of soft leather bags.

"Hey, Vanita let's look in here," I said grabbing her arm as she prepared to dodge the traffic and cross the street.

"Here we go again," she exclaimed, a trifle exasperated by my constant stopping to look at the treasure trove of crafts that appeared to be everywhere.

"Just five minutes," I replied darting into the small shop which was filled with scores of bags hanging from the walls and piled on the floor.

"Welcome to my shop," the shopkeeper said as he suddenly appeared sporting a large black moustache and a beaming smile. "How can I help you?"

Smiling back at him, I replied, "You have such a wonderful collection of handbags. I'd like to look around."

"Please do and while you are looking, let me offer you some refreshments."

Before we had a chance to reply he called out, "Anil."

A young boy appeared from the back of the store. The shopkeeper said something quietly to him and the boy disappeared again to reappear a few minutes later with a silver tray holding three glasses of mint tea. Not wanting to appear rude, we each took a glass and a sip.

"Thank you. This is very refreshing," said Vanita who had managed to find a chair near the entrance and, realizing how long a "five minutes" this was going to be, was making herself comfortable.

I, meanwhile, wandered into the many alcoves in the shop and the shopkeeper followed me. He pulled out more and more leather bags decorated with beautiful embroidery from hidden corners. The soft leathers, in all their colors and shapes, were gorgeous. I wanted them all. I was paralyzed by indecision brought on by an overload of choice. Bags like these in England were few and far between and they were really expensive.

The floor was now covered in bags and I was standing knee deep in the middle of them with the shopkeeper looking increasingly puzzled by my inability to make a decision.

"Madam does not see a bag she likes?"

"Yes. They are all so lovely. It's just so difficult to decide which one to take."

The shopkeeper stood there thinking for a moment. Then his face lit up with a beam of inspiration and he said, "Wait here."

He disappeared into the back of the shop. A few minutes later, he reappeared with a flourish, holding his prize high in the air.

"Here it is. I have just the bag for you. It's the only one in the shop. It's very special and very different."

He looked alarmed as both Vanita and I started shaking with laughter at the bag he was holding.

His masterpiece, the most expensive item in the shop, was a boring looking black plastic handbag, the type usually piled high in department stores. To reach Srinagar it had traveled by plane and truck and being rare and imported was understandably expensive. Indeed, here in Kashmir, it was probably a much sought after item being so different from the everyday plentiful local leather bags that were so prized in the west.

Here, in a nutshell, was a lesson in scarcity of goods economics.

"We must stop laughing and apologize to the shopkeeper," Vanita said quietly. "We have obviously hurt his feelings."

I nodded in agreement.

"Thank you very much for showing me this bag," I said, "but it's your wonderful local leather handbags that I want. They are all so lovely that it has made it difficult to decide which ones I want to choose. But now I have made up my mind."

The shopkeeper still looked unconvinced, but cheered up noticeably as I selected my five favorite bags to buy.

Smiling, as he packed them for me, he said, "Come back tomorrow and I will bring more bags."

I grinned and said, "Thank you. We would like to, but we can't. Tomorrow we are going pony trekking in the mountains."

Pony Trekking in the Himalayas

"Right leg or left?" I asked, looking at the pony who looked right back at me with a haughty air and a slightly puzzled look in his big brown eyes.

You could almost hear him saying, *does this crazy clueless English woman think she can have a conversation with me, a sure-footed pony of the Himalayas, just like that? Doesn't she understand the etiquette of these hills and that she needs to approach me via my handler? That's the way it's done here. Still, she's a tourist so what can you expect?*

He tossed his head and looked away with a hint of distain gazing into the dreamy distance of ice cream snowcaps.

"Right leg or left?" I repeated obviously not expecting an answer, but somehow needing the reassurance of saying it.

The reason that I was being so unduly cautious was that my last experience of mounting an animal, albeit a donkey, had been as a seven-year-old, in the English seaside town of Ramsgate.

Then, I had chosen to ride the only neurotic donkey on the beach. He apparently had an aversion to leather and as soon as I had clambered aboard, he had spotted a woman with a leather bag and had bolted. I was thrown off in the process and dragged howling along by my right foot. Amazingly, only my pride was hurt and nothing else.

So you see this new adventure many years later in a very different land, high in the foothills of the Himalayas, was being approached with some understandable trepidation.

We were about to embark on a pony trek over ice bridges to Chandanwadi, a scenic glacier nine thousand feet up in the Himalayas and had driven from Srinagar to Pahalgam early that morning to start our trek.

"Look. This is how you do it, Vivien," Vanita yelled, appearing to leap up.

"Show off," I retorted, watching the other members of the group mount more cautiously using upturned crates. My pony was now being held by one of the young handlers Rahil, who gave me a big grin and held out his hand to help me. Somewhat clumsily, I managed to get myself into the saddle.

"Ready?" shouted Samir, our guide.

"Yes," we replied in an excited chorus and we were off, swaying out of the stable yard and onto a mud path. To my relief, I saw all the ponies were being led by youthful handlers.

The mountain air was crisp and fresh as the line of ponies began to climb up steep paths. In the lead was Samir, followed by Vanita's mother looking regal and elegant in her light green silk sari. She was followed by Vanita and me. Bringing up the rear was Prakash, a family friend accompanying us on this part of our adventure.

Clip clop, clip clop, the ponies hoofs beat out a hypnotic rhythm as we climbed higher and higher out of the Liddar Valley, the rhythm only broken by the sound of disturbed pebbles falling into the fast receding river far below. High above us, a golden eagle floated on the air currents lazily perusing the scene looking for a tasty lunch.

"Look, Look! There they are, the ice bridges," Vanita's voice floated back to me carried on currents of the fresh invigorating air.

We had arrived at the point where it was necessary to cross the canyon. There was normally no way across, as the canyon had no

Eyeballing Big Croc

bridge at this location, but for a few brief winter and early spring months, it was possible to use the compacted ice that formed an ice bridge over the narrow gorge. In summer, these ice bridges melted.

This was going to be both exhilarating and terrifying. What if my pony stumbled and I fell off? It was a long way down.

The ponies in front of me slowly and sure-footedly walked onto the ice. They weren't perturbed by the crossing, so why should I be? I felt my tenseness ease as I waited my turn and took in the beautiful and majestic views of the green alpine valley and snowcapped mountain peaks. Was I really sitting here on a pony in this amazing place?

Lulled by the serenity of my surroundings, I was expecting the steady pace to continue, when suddenly I felt a jolt and a rush of cold air as my pony decided to cross this first of the ice bridges in a flying gallop that sent my sunglasses bouncing over my head and nearly disposed of me down the aforementioned gorge.

What is it with four legged animals and me? I wondered. *Was my pony getting even for something he did not like about me? Perhaps he did not approve of me trying to speak to him earlier?* Rahil, who had looked momentarily surprised, grinned at me reassuringly as he steadied the pony.

"Did you enjoy that?" laughed Vanita as she looked back.

"Yes," I stuttered, gasping and trying to catch my breath.

Actually I had. With my adrenalin pumping and the danger now past, I realized that I had enjoyed the sheer exhilaration of it, a thrill beyond words. Roller coasters had nothing on this. What a buzz and what a story for future telling.

Our trek continued along the winding steep paths and more ice bridges, (with crossings now more carefully controlled by the pony handlers) onward and upward climbing in the crisp wine-like air past pine forests and roaring rivers.

And then we were there. When arriving at Chandanwadi, it was a delight to have a picnic lunch surrounded by snowcapped peaks and then to skate on the glacier and toboggan down its steep side and watch the brilliantly white ice suddenly melt into a frothing spring.

Here in the heart of the mountains, I absorbed the scene not just visually, but through a process of osmosis, a waking of all the senses, to the sheer magnificence of this amazing world of which we are so privileged to be a part.

A Day in Tehran

The shimmering multicolored dancing lights of the diamonds were hypnotic and were gradually pulling me towards their alluring brilliance. I was entranced.

Suddenly, I became aware of noise and shouting. A uniformed security guard had pushed his way through the crowd of people standing next to me and was yelling at me in Farsi. I didn't understand a word he was saying.

Our museum guide quickly and urgently translated for me in accented English, obviously diplomatically softening his angry words.

"He is asking you to step back from the protective barrier or it will trigger an alarm that will activate an immediate shut down of the vault and we will all be locked in."

There was an anxious murmur from the other visitors in the display vault who were all staring at me, as I pulled my gaze away from the fiery allure of the diamonds. I moved back, remembering the events that had brought me to this enticing museum vault.

I had just spent ten weeks on vacation in India visiting Vanita, a Sussex University friend, who had challenged a group of us, when we graduated, to come to India and look beyond the stereotypes. I had been the only one to accept; it was just too good an opportunity to miss.

It had been an eye-opening experience. I had pony trekked across ice bridges in the foothills of the Himalayas, hobnobbed with a prince and politicians, eyeballed a crocodile and stayed in palaces. I had also observed the difficulties and hopes of everyday life in this vast and fascinating country. Now my visit was coming to an end.

"This has been a really amazing experience," I said to Vanita, as we strolled towards the offices of Air India in Bombay to confirm my return flight. "I wish it could just go on and on."

"Well it can't," replied Vanita, ever the pragmatist. "However, you might want to try for an extra free day on your return journey."

I looked at her blankly not understanding, "What do you mean?" I asked, as we entered the Air India offices.

"Come on, I'll show you," she replied with a grin, as we approached the counter. She was an experienced world traveler and I decided to watch her in action.

"Good morning ladies. How can I be of assistance?" asked the neatly uniformed travel clerk.

"Good morning," we chorused back.

"My friend has just spent ten weeks exploring India," Vanita began, "and now wants to reconfirm her return flight. She has an Air India ticket to Iran where she will catch a connecting BOAC flight to Israel. She would really like the opportunity to see Tehran and was wondering if you could possibly arrange for that to happen?"

The ticket clerk smiled and, looking at me, said, "Well let me have your passport and return ticket and I will see what I can do."

After a few minutes checking flights, he said, "There is a seat on an Air India flight leaving Bombay early tomorrow morning Wednesday, June 25, arriving in Tehran just after the connecting BOAC flight to Tel Aviv has left. I can however book you on the 9:00 a.m. BOAC flight to Tel Aviv the following day. Will that suit you?"

"Yes, please," I answered quickly, delighted at this unexpected opportunity to spend a day exploring Tehran.

"And of course you will provide a complimentary hotel in central Tehran for the night," interrupted Vanita, ever the consummate traveler. After all, these were the days when flying was both an adventure and a pleasure.

"Yes, of course" was the reply. "Have a good flight," he said as he handed me my flight tickets and a hotel voucher.

"See," said Vanita with a big grin as we left.

"Thanks," I beamed back.

As the plane circled Tehran the next morning preparing to land, I could see sun baked fields and mud colored villages backed by the snowcapped peaks of the Tochal Mountains. They contrasted strangely with the high-rise buildings of the approaching modern city.

At Mehrabad Airport, a taxi was waiting for me and some fellow passengers who were also catching connections the next day. As we drove into Tehran, we passed groups of students with placards standing outside the railings of some official looking buildings.

"What's going on?" I asked the driver.

"It's the students," he replied, "they are protesting against the Shah and his policies. It's been going on for days. Every day more students turn up."

In the lobby, waiting to check in at the hotel, I started to chat to Subhash, an Indian student and Olivia, a traveler from Australia and we decided to explore Tehran together. For several hours we just wandered around the city, first the wide streets with their modern shops and then down the side streets and alleyways into the Grand Bazaar alive with crowds, colors and spices. Stalls piled high with fruit and vegetables, copper and brass ornaments, bright delicately flowered ceramics and mounds of deliciously aromatic spices, burnished gold, ambers, rusts and browns all piled high.

We wandered into the courtyards of blue domed mosques with their intricately designed minarets and their brilliantly distinctive ornamental tiles and fountains. Many women were wearing western dress, but even those women wearing the more traditional chador, were clothed in light colored flower printed materials, not heavy dark colors.

After some time, we were tempted to stop for some sweet pastries and strong refreshing Turkish coffee and Subhash and Olivia decided that they just wanted to sit and watch the world meander by for a while.

I meanwhile, had very different plans. There was something I just had to see before I left the city. There was no way I was going to leave Tehran without seeing the famed Crown Jewels of the Shah. They were housed in the museum display vaults at Bank Markazi, The Central Bank of Iran and the hotel had given me directions to its location.

So here I was, gazing mesmerized by the display of diamonds, emeralds, rubies, sapphires and pearls embedded in the crowns, tiaras and thrones of the Shah dynasty, when the voice of the museum guide interrupted my thoughts saying, "Ladies and gentlemen, the museum vault will be closing in five minutes. We need to leave or we will be locked in for the night."

Fire and ice shimmied like lasers off the diamonds and multitude of jewels, as I turned to go. Emerging from the bank, I stood still on the bustling Tehran Street, momentarily dazzled, this time by the sparkling golden rays of a brilliant sunset.

Six Days In June

I was soaked. I stood there in the kibbutz kitchen with water dripping from my hair, down my neck and onto my jeans. My large white plastic apron had deflected some of the greasy splash and was now channeling rivulets of soapy suds back into the giant sink and down into my well worn flip-flops.

Just beyond the hatch to the sink in the kibbutz dining room, I could hear the sound of suppressed laughter as a mischievous ten-year-old Amir whispered to his friend Alon in a very conspicuous voice, "We got her, we got her. I told you we would."

They had indeed. After several days of trying unsuccessfully to flip the dirty dishes into the huge washing up sink dam buster's style, today the spin had caught me, their English teacher, standing in the crucial maximum splash area.

"Careful you don't slip," laughed John as water dripped onto the floor.

He was a volunteer from London working alongside me in the kitchen clearing up after lunch and had managed to avoid the deluge of water and stay dry. He grinned as he said in his cockney accent, "Cheeky little buggers aren't they?"

"Yes they are," I agreed, "but somehow it's reassuring that they can still act as normal mischievous kids after everything that has happened today."

My mind flashed back to the day's events, for though today had started as usual, it had been anything but normal.

It had been a beautiful sunny morning as I meandered towards the small kibbutz school. Birds were chirping in the trees that canopied the shady paths and the green lawns were surrounded by colorful blooming flowers. Life began early in the kibbutz, to avoid the heat of the day, and though school started at 8:00 a.m. the tractors had been at work for several hours in the cotton, corn and sugar beet fields. The shaded citrus groves were busy with members tending the juicy oranges, lemons and grapefruits, while pears, peaches, apricots and apples were being picked by sleep-eyed volunteers who partied late into the night in the wooden huts they shared, yet somehow managed to fall out of bed at the crack of dawn to work. In the morning quiet, the gentle breeze carried the distant sounds of clucking chickens and the mooing and baas of sheep and cattle grazing in the fields.

In such a peaceful setting, it was easy to lose focus about the dangers that were constantly escalating beyond the kibbutz gates regarding the political situation in the Middle East. Volunteers were arriving each day from around the world to help with the work of the kibbutz, as members were being called to the army reserves in the face of Israel's neighbors threat of invasion. The mood was somber, with people uncertain what was going to happen.

I had come to Kibbutz Hasolelim as a part-time English teacher, following a short course in Hebrew in the desert town of Beersheba. I was also helping out in a variety of jobs in the kitchen, picking fruit and herding sheep. Just yesterday, I had worked with a group of volunteers filling sandbags to put under the houses to afford some measure of protection should hostilities start. It was not exactly a job I was experienced in and I was fervently hoping that the corner I had built would not fall down.

As I walked towards the classroom, I noticed something strange. It was so quiet. Something was missing. Where were the yells and shouts that could usually be heard on the pathway? Opening the classroom door, I immediately saw the class was grouped around a small radio. They turned it off as soon as they noticed me and moved to their seats.

"Boker Tov–Good morning." I said putting my books on the desk and glancing around to make sure everyone was in class. "Let's begin by talking about the situation." I started to write the word in English on the blackboard.

"No," shouted fourteen-year-old Naaman "It's milhama-war."

My hand jerked to a stop. I turned around and said, careful to translate the words into Hebrew, "No Naaman. It's still a situation, not a war."

Whereupon the whole class yelled back in Hebrew, "No it's not a situation! It's war! We have just heard it on the radio. Listen."

They turned it on and they were right. It was June 5 1967 and the Six-Day War had just begun and life in the region would never be the same again.

Part 2: Disjointed notes written during the period of the Six-Day War June 1967 at Kibbutz Hasolelim.

The 'O' certainly jumped out of 'homework' today when planes flew overhead during the English lesson. It was the sudden noise. A quick glance at the class and back again to the blackboard, reassured me that it hadn't bounced as high as I first feared.

I'm feeling really nervous tonight. It's the thought of undiscriminating bombs and artillery just dropping and destroying anything in their path. My British international peaceful student consciousness has not prepared me for such thoughts.

Worked in the cemetery today watering plants with a thin green plastic hose and clipping off dead rosebuds. It's a beautiful place, a part of nature, a quiet resting place for two kibbutz members. I tried to push away obvious thoughts.

Must get on with my marking. As usual, I have left it until the last moment.

Anat noticed the irony of the situation yesterday. Instead of meeting my eldest pupils in the classroom, I'm now working with them in the kibbutz. Yona fixed a leaking sink, while Anat and Ora worked on the food trolleys. Amira washed dishes with me, helped and heckled by several younger members of the school.

It's weed clearing and sandbag day today. One of the things I have always found most attractive about Kibbutz Hasolelim is the wildness and freedom of its gardens. There's always an element of surprise in the combination of shapes and colors waving in the gentle breezes against the blue sky and glistening with beads of moisture from the water sprinklers. It's such a contrast to some other kibbutzim I have visited where every blade of grass has its correct and organized place. It's a continuing theme for me, as in England I always preferred the wildness of the sea and open countryside to the controlled symmetry of London's parks.

Today, however, some of the wildness had to be sacrificed. If, as seems likely, hostilities are about to break out, the kibbutz has to minimize the possibility of fire. So from dawn to dusk today everyone available has been working weeding, cutting and raking plants, flowers and branches away from the houses.

The other main activity today has been piling sandbags under various buildings on stilts. I had thought the idea was to support the buildings if the foundations were shaken by any blasts, but apparently not. The purpose is to provide protection from flying shrapnel. At every building where the sandbags have appeared, so have the children to play new games in the strange surroundings. Their childish shouts contrast strangely with the taunt and tired bodies of the seventeen and eighteen-year-old boys working on this physically exhausting job, their newly developed muscles glistening with sweat as they work in the blazing sun.

I worked with some of the girls for a couple of hours on the relatively easy task of shoveling sand into the sandbags, but a volunteer student, a mathematician from The Hebrew University of Jerusalem obviously not used to physical work was literally shaking from exhaustion after seven hours of this backbreaking work.

June 5, 1967. This morning hostilities commenced between Israel, Egypt, Syria and Jordan. I found out in the most startling way. Nellie, the class teacher requested that I allow the class to listen to the nine o'clock news. I agreed thinking nothing strange about it. I then commenced the English lesson planning to give out newspaper topics for a project later in the week, adding that obviously the Middle East situation would take a central point. Naa'man then proceeded to select the topic of "the war" which I corrected to "the situation" to be corrected in turn by a quarter of the class who assured me Israel was, at that time 8:40 a.m. in a state of war.

I seem to have accepted this in a surprisingly calm way. Whatever I had hoped deep down, I had not believed that the issue would be settled without fighting. I am one hundred percent committed to Israel's cause, believing as I do in her right to exist.

The most noticeable difference today has been the shadow accompanying every kibbutz member: his or her radio. Every hour, as news time approaches, there is an expectant hush as everyone stops to hear what's happening.

Spent about an hour in a shelter today which is a sandbag-protected space under a children's house. Felt two strong vibrations as a bomb was dropped in the vicinity.

What a curious land of contrasts Israel is. Only a week ago, the country was in a state of declared war, with fighting on the borders, populations of towns living in shelters and kibbutzim under fire. Now just a week later, the war has been decisively concluded on the military front and Israel's position dramatically strengthened to the amazement of the world. Now starts the long process of diplomatic bargaining.

Sing a Song of Soldiers

Sing a song of soldiers,
the students silent grew,
beneath the arc of light and noise,
a fearful nerve still throbs.

"My soldier has returned to me,"
folked the off key voice,
as feeling eyes read faces,
and mouths kissed present lips.

>   Students Union,
>   Tel Aviv University. 8/23/1968.

Fragments

Seven o'clock,
and a small sparrow
pecks
at a dry crust in a tarmac courtyard.

Nearby,
two Arabic chattering
uzzied guards,
stroll along the fenced perimeter
of the student village.

Suddenly,
swooping low,
a bird quivers
over a patch of
red poppies
in the silent cemetery.

Silhouetted,
against a Dead Sea
skyline,
(undulating desert
and flashing blue)
a boy goatherd
tends his scrawny
flock of goats,
while toiling at
the fragments of a recent lesson.

Heralded by a
steady clomp,
an elderly villager
"aboard"
a swaying donkey
ambles past
lighting a pipe.

Morning,
slowly and sunnily
meanders
towards ten.

2/14/1970. Har Hatzofim. (Mount Scopus) Jerusalem.

Eilat

At the tip of the desert,
crinkled mountains,
(pink-purple in the setting sun)
enfold
a blue, blue bay of water.

In the center of town,
pedestrians duck,
as planes
hum down,
on a patch of space,
labeled,
"airport."

At the Egged bus station,
(a mud field and a shed)
Eilat,
nonchalantly surveys
the latest batch
of legs,
as they emerge
from roaring buses.

At the waters edge,
a flabby varicosed
backside,
patterned
by the briefest
of bikinis.

Grouped,
at "Maurice's,"
the hippies
sit, talk and smoke,
while boney dogs,
chase
scraps of nothing.

Meanwhile,
three stories up,
behind fluted blinds,
an arched thirty-three
year old neck
is glimpsed,
anxiously,
awaiting the arrival
of her twenty-year-old
soldier.

Much later,
(as trucks thunder to Timna)
at the "Half Past Midnight,"
over iced coffee
and falafel,
Eilat watches
twinkling Aqaba,
and the world go by.

The Soldier from the Kibbutz

The morning mist rose steamily from the desert floor as the rays of sunlight touched everything with sparkling light. Perched high on an outcrop of rock, a figure sat mesmerized by the sheer beauty of the morning's awakening in this desert arena. To one side, the proud outline of Herod's fortress was etched against the now brilliant blue sky, an eternal symbol of Jewish defiance and hope.

Climbing the snake path to reach the summit earlier that day in the pre-dawn darkness had awakened a sense of awe and wonder, an awareness of the bravery and sacrifice of the 960 defenders of Masada, the Jewish rebels, men, woman and children who committed mass suicide in 74 CE rather than be captured by the Romans. She had felt a need to lose the crowd of other visitors and find a quiet place to just sit and absorb everything.

Suddenly, a sound distracted her and she became aware of a young soldier standing on a terrace above her. He seemed to be staring at her.

"So what," she thought, she wasn't doing anything wrong. She turned her gaze back to the beauty of the morning and the view of the Judean Desert, catching sight of a steady stream of ant-like figures making their way up the path.

Her thoughts were again disturbed by the noise of some falling stones as the soldier slid down the slope and there he was, standing right next to her with cropped hair and a young fresh barely shaved face. Silver paratrooper wings glinted on his olive colored uniform and an Uzi was casually slung over his shoulder.

"What had she done? Was he about to arrest her?" she wondered. "Perhaps taking photos was not allowed here."

"Shalom. Isn't this a beautiful view?" the soldier said in accented English.

"Yes, stunning," she agreed, relaxing a bit. He obviously was not going to arrest her, but what did he really want? She looked at him quizzically.

What followed came like a bolt out of the blue.

"Do you have a sister named Vivien?"

She looked at him in total astonishment. She had never seen this complete stranger before and didn't have a clue who he was or where he came from and he was asking about her sister. She did in fact have a sister called Vivien who was five years older than her, but she had blond hair and blue eyes and in no way resembled her. She herself was Mediterranean looking, often taken for Spanish with olive skin, brown eyes and curly hair. How could he possibly connect them?

The soldier observing the surprised expression on her face repeated his question. "Do you have a sister named Vivien?" "Yes," she replied reluctantly after a slight hesitation, "But how do you know?"

He grinned and a big smile spread across his face. "Vivien was my English teacher two years ago in 1968 at Kibbutz Kfar Szold. You look just like her. Isn't my English good?"

"But we look nothing alike! "Everybody always remarks on our different appearances."

"That's not right," the soldier replied, "as soon as I noticed you sitting on the rock I saw the family resemblance and recognized you. What's your name?"

"Avril."

"Well I'm Gaby. Na'im me'od, nice to meet you. Now I must get back to my unit. Say that Gaby sends greetings next time you see Vivien and tell her I'm now a paratrooper. Goodbye."

With that, he climbed back up the terrace and disappeared over the ridge, leaving her sitting there totally bemused. After a few minutes, she began to see the humorous side of the encounter and started to laugh.

A dawn visit to a place of beauty and connection to her Jewish roots had made her aware, completely out of the blue, of a family resemblance that until that moment, she had no idea existed and that no one had seen before. She couldn't wait to tell the story to her sister and family.

Skype Me

"Skype me." The email arrived out of the blue.

Glancing through my emails, I had almost missed this one and was about to bin it as junk without opening it. It had been such a long time. Why now?

Then I remembered the reunion that had taken place in Israel just a few weeks earlier to celebrate my friend Gill's birthday. She had decided on the spur of the moment to invite a group of friends to a party in Jerusalem where she now lived. As new graduates, we had spent a year together in Israel in 1967 studying Hebrew and volunteering. At such short notice, I had been unable to make the trip. Gill must have given him my email.

I immediately clicked onto Facebook. Forty years was a long time to be out of touch with somebody and I was in need of some refreshing clues if I was to reply.

Now sitting here in sunny California in 2013 I was staring at his photo on Facebook. Head to one side with slack jaw, pleasant face smiling like a kindly uncle, rather than the tall angular youth whose image I had summoned from the archives of my memory.

Looking at the photo of a family tableau taken in Tel Aviv where he now lived with his wife and daughters, I imagined, what the family dynamics would have been and what the children would have looked like, if I had been standing beside him in that photograph. An amusing, but totally pointless exercise.

"Did I really want to Skype him?"

Suddenly the memory of a warm Jerusalem evening flashed to mind, taking me back to 1967. During our time there, "The Six-Day War," had occurred. I was teaching on Kibbutz Hasolelim in Lower Galilee and Leon was working as a statistician in The Ministry of Economics in Jerusalem. With the cessation of hostilities, our group had come together for a few days in Jerusalem.

It was a busy time in the now reunited city with a flurry of activity as dividing barriers were dismantled and the circle of mines surrounding the city was disarmed. Just that afternoon, we had watched from a safe distance as army sappers capped and blew up some mines near the soon-to-be-dismantled Mandelbaum Gate.

On the evening before I was due to return to the kibbutz, Leon and I decided to meet without the rest of the group for a more intimate dinner at a restaurant in Jaffa Road. Leon arrived looking excited.

"I've just heard at the ministry that the curfew is being lifted on the Old City tonight, and it's going to be publicly announced tomorrow. But tonight very few people know."

"Let's go and explore when we finish eating."

Who could resist? At last, the chance to walk freely in the reunited city.

The memories of that evening still linger. I remember vividly the echo of our footsteps down silent deserted shadowed alleyways. The awareness of scores of invisible eyes watching silently from behind shuttered windows showing chinks of light. Residents wondering what the peace would bring, how it would affect their every day lives. How would the inhabitants of East and West Jerusalem interact?

It was impossible to know. We had entered a new and changing world. As we meandered through the tangle of winding alleyways, the only sound was the occasional meow of a cat as it scurried out of our way.

As I sat at my computer lost in my recollections, I heard a sudden bleep. My Skype was ringing. My hand hovered. Perhaps now was the time to catch up and compare notes about our lives during the intervening years?

Do You Remember Esther?

"Do you remember Esther?" My friend Gill asked as she pushed open the door of the optician's shop in downtown Jerusalem.

I looked at her blankly, wondering why she was asking me such a strange question.

Suddenly, as if in a dream, I found myself floating in warm turquoise waters. I could see reeds swaying in the distance and they appeared to be beckoning me to come closer. As I drew nearer, everything suddenly changed as they whirled towards me, their long stems wrapping around my ankles and pulling me down.

As I fought to break free, I opened my eyes and realized that they were not reeds, but a forest of hairy muscular legs —dozens of them towering above me— as I lay sprawled on the burning hot uncomfortable pebbles of the Dead Sea beach.

My very brief bikini felt as if it had retreated from the vital areas it was supposed to cover and I had the strange taste of hard-boiled eggs on my lips. Close by, I could hear the gentle flow of a freshwater stream, while the question "Do you remember Esther?" seemed to be reverberating faintly in the distance.

What was happening? Had I fallen down a rabbit hole? Was that why everything seemed so distorted?

"Look! She's opened her eyes," a voice above me announced to the surrounding legs. "She appears to be okay. Let's move back and give her some more air. The show's over."

As I focused my eyes, I saw the bright ginger hair of my friend Gill.

"How are you feeling?" she asked.

"What happened? Why am I sprawled out on the beach like this?"

"You need to thank Motti."

"But why?"

"Well, he just pulled you out of the stream."

I suddenly remembered feeling really hot in the blazing heat of the Dead Sea where I was spending the day in the summer of 1972 with a group of friends from Jerusalem. I had decided to go and sit in the cooling waters of a nearby freshwater stream. As I waded in, the bottom had felt slimy and I had slipped and fallen down really hard on a rock in the middle of the stream.

Gill continued, "Suddenly Motti, who was in the middle of eating a hard-boiled egg sandwich, leapt up, dropped his sandwich and went running into the stream. Nobody else had noticed, but he had seen you fall backwards into the water. Jumping in, he pulled you out, and even gave you mouth to mouth. So you see, you really need to thank him for saving you."

The forest of legs had dispersed as Motti put out his hand to help me back on my feet. I hurriedly adjusted my bikini to cover what it was designed to do. Motti stood there with egg crumbs on his unshaven cheeks looking sheepish. I flung my arms around his neck in a grateful hug.

The loud jangle of a bell as somebody pushed open the optician's door, disturbed my thoughts and brought me back to the present which was some forty years later. It was August 2014 and I now lived in San Francisco, and was on a visit to see family and friends in Israel.

"Well do you remember Esther?" Gill repeated.

Eyeballing Big Croc

I again looked at her blankly,
"Because she remembers you."
As we approached the counter, a woman greeted Gill.
"Shalom, how are things?"
"Hello, Esther. This is Vivien. Do you remember her?"
Esther smiled slowly and said," Of course I do. She's the person my husband Motti pulled from the stream at the Dead Sea all those years ago."

As the door of the opticians shop jangled close, I looked around. Standing there was somebody I instantly recognized, a thickset man with curly brownish hair and a thick bushy beard amply flecked with grey. He was biting into a falafel and pita sandwich, which he was obviously enjoying.

"Are you ready to go Esther, I'm double parked?"
"Yes I'm ready, but look who is visiting from America. Do you remember her?"

As I turned to greet him, he gave me a big grin, took a bite from his falafel sandwich, and said, "Hi Vivien. How are you doing?"

Dressing Up

It was a blazing hot afternoon in August 2014 in Modi'in, a town located between Jerusalem and Tel Aviv and, famous as the place where the Maccabean revolt began in 160 BCE against the Seleucid Greeks. The balcony door was open and the distant Judean Hills shimmered in the heat, framing the gently swaying branches of the pomegranate and passiflora trees in the garden below.

I was sprawled on the sofa, my eyelids drooping, having managed just a few pages of my John Grisham book. The room was surprisingly quiet, after some previous rowdy play. I was visiting my cousin Hadassah and her five children for a few days while on vacation from my home in San Francisco and my ears had grown accustomed to the melody and rising crescendo of children's voices.

For the moment though, everybody was quietly engaged. Itai, aged nine, was playing a board game featuring submarines with his brother Nadav, aged seven. Sharon, aged thirteen, was in her bedroom on her computer, while Anov, aged eleven, was helping her mother Hadassah assemble a bookshelf purchased at Ikea the day before. The only energetic activity was that of Yuval, a sturdy three-year-old, who was jumping up and down from an alcove on the stairs, using a very long clean bandage as a rope.

Suddenly, I became aware of a change of activity in the room. The board game appeared finished and Itai was whispering something to Nadav who nodded his head.

Both boys then began moving quietly towards the front door. Yuval stopped his jumping and rushed after them as they opened the door. I could hear their footsteps clattering down the stone steps. They were probably going to play outside in the courtyard. In the distance, a door banged shut.

I picked up my book and started to read again. However, before very long, I was distracted by the sound of thumping, as if something very heavy was being dragged up the steps. Sure enough, the door opened and Itai entered dragging a large navy duffle bag. Nadav and Yuval were pushing it from behind. Not a word was uttered as the three boys pushed the bag to the center of the room, and Itai silently unzipped it. The silence was unnerving. What were they doing?

As I watched, Itai began pulling a blue uniform and beret out of the bag. It was obviously that of an adult, yet he began putting on the shirt. When he had finished buttoning it up, he put on the blue beret. Nadov, meanwhile, had taken a beige uniform and cap from the bag and was doing exactly the same thing. Not to be outdone, Yuval pulled out a blue shirt which he slowly put on, not attempting to button it up. He stood there looking so cute with the shirt reaching the floor and sleeves that were twice the length of his arms. Kids playing at dressing up; what a photo opportunity!

As I reached for my camera, my hand suddenly froze, as I realized in horror what I was actually witnessing. This was no childish game; these were children dealing with unimaginable trauma.

Just four months earlier, the family had set out in the late afternoon to drive from Modi'in to Kiryat Arba to enjoy a family Pesach Seder with Hadassah's parents.

As they were driving along, a motorcycle with two riders suddenly appeared and, without any warning the riders started shooting at the car which was struck by forty-six bullets. Baruch, their father, had spotted the impending attack and had yelled at the four children in the car to get down on the floor. As he tried to accelerate to save his family, he was struck by bullets and instantly killed. As Hadassah turned towards him, two bullets hit her in the back, fortunately missing her vital organs.

Amazingly, she kept calm and with Baruch's foot still jammed on the accelerator, she managed to grab the steering wheel and miraculously keep the car on the road to avoid crashing. Incredibly, she succeeded in outrunning the terrorists who fled as she reached the safety of an army outpost.

The children had escaped physical injury, but had seen and heard everything. They were immediately rushed from the scene by their rescuers as their mother received medical attention. However, they were traumatized by what they had witnessed. In a few moments, their young lives had changed forever.

Now as I watched in stunned silence, Itai raised his arm in a silent salute to his father, followed by Nadov and then by little Yuval. They then marched around the coffee table three times in their father's clothes without uttering a sound. Then they stopped and silently took off the clothes, folded them and stuffed them back into the duffle bag.

Itai immediately zipped it up and all three began dragging it back towards the door. Opening the door, they began the reverse procedure of slowly dragging it downstairs. The only sound to be heard was the thumping noise it made as if they were beating a sad retreat.

I was left sitting there overwhelmed with tears running down my cheeks, having witnessed this heartbreaking scene, its memory etched forever. No child should ever have to deal with, what these three young boys had endured.

But then with amazing resilience, the door burst open and three boisterous boys came dashing in shouting and yelling. Yuval went into the kitchen and, dragging a chair up to the fridge, climbed up and opened the top freezer and took out three popsicles. Climbing down, he opened one and handed the others to his brothers. Then they rushed out onto the balcony to play.

Fearlessly Facing Little Croc

I looked up at my mummy and daddy and chuckled as I sat on the carpet, fearlessly facing little croc, my new friend.

It had been an ordinary morning in May 1945 until I suddenly heard a loud voice say,

"Come to Uncle."

Uncle? What's an uncle?

I glanced up momentarily distracted from playing with the little piggies in my playpen. Now I knew what "little piggies" were: there was one who went to market, another who liked roast beef and one, like me, who stayed at home. Mummy told me all about them every night before I went to sleep. *But an Uncle? What was that?*

"Come to uncle," boomed the hairy green monster standing by my playpen. He was very tall and had what looked like mummy's hairbrush under his nose. He gave a sudden laugh and I saw he had big white teeth. He looked just like the giant in the story mummy had read to me in "Jack and the Beanstalk."

Was he hungry? Did he want to eat me up?

I was scared and felt tears start to run down my cheeks, when suddenly I heard the soft voice of my lovely mummy. She reached down and gently stroked my golden hair.

"Now Monty darling. This is your daughter, Vivien. You're not her uncle. You're her daddy. She doesn't know you, so don't frighten her. Speak softly."

Bending down, she lifted me out of the playpen wiping away my tears.

"Look, Vivvy, don't be frightened. This is your daddy. He's come home from the war to see you."

Now, that was different. "Daddy" was a word I definitely knew as every night Mummy would sing me a song about my "daddy coming home from the war."

I stopped crying and looked at him with interest.

The green giant now named "Daddy" reached out and gently took me from mummy.

His arms felt strong and his olive-green jacket was scratchy. Mummy always felt soft and gentle and smelled like peaches and custard, but Daddy smelt of outside and apples and oatmeal.

He put his face close to mine saying, "Hello, Vivien. I'm your daddy. I've waited nine long months to meet you."

He gently kissed me and the soft brush under his nose tickled my cheek.

With his other arm, he reached out to include mummy in an all-embracing hug saying, "Now that I'm home from the army, we can be a real family together at last."

As he held us in a close embrace, I noticed that he had a large beige canvas army duffle bag slung across his shoulder.

"Look Vivvy, I've brought a present for you," he said, handing me back to mummy.

A present? What's that? Another new word. What did that mean?

He swung the bag off his shoulder and it landed on the floor with a thud. Bending down he started to pull things out of it: rolled up shirts, vests and socks.

Were those presents?

Obviously not because he continued piling what looked like mummy's dirty washing onto the floor. Suddenly, he triumphantly pulled out a package wrapped in brown paper and tied with string.

Eyeballing Big Croc

"Here it is!"

I looked at him with surprise in my big blue eyes. *Was that big brown bag a present? It looked just like the bag mummy brought back from the grocer's shop. What was so special about that?*

He must have seen the bewilderment in my eyes because he laughed and said, "Wait until you see this."

He ripped off the brown paper wrapping and I saw a funny looking creature looking at me. It had bulging eyes and was olive green with a rough and bumpy skin. It had a very long nose and a smiley mouth with white painted teeth. At the end of each of its four short legs were bright red wheels. There was a ring attached to its funny nose with a colorful string tied to it.

I looked at mummy for some type of reassurance and saw that she was smiling at it, and looked really happy so it could not be anything to be frightened of.

"Where did you get it Monty?" she asked. "Toys are so difficult to find now with all the shortages after the war."

"Lance, one of the men in my unit made it. Look it's carved in five separate sections and they all move when you pull it along."

He pulled the string and the little monster moved from side to side as the red wheels turned.

"Oh how nice. I must write and thank him and invite him for dinner."

"Look at this Vivvy," she said as she put me down on the carpet with a big smile on her face. She gave a small tug on the string and the crocodile swayed from side to side, moving closer to me. "Now you try."

I looked up at my mummy and daddy and then chuckled as I reached for the string, fearlessly facing little croc, my first real toy.

Many years later, while traveling in India, I came face-to-face with a real croc in a lake on the estate of the Maharaja of Baroda. That thrilling encounter took me back many years as I remembered the day my father came home from the war.

A Kaleidoscope of Colors

The negotiations began in earnest on the staircase after tea as the adults chatted in the dining room. On one side was Clive, my ten-year-old cousin, rosy-cheeked with brown soaped-down hair, a white open-necked shirt and short grey trousers, displaying a jauntily placed Band-Aid over a scraped knee. I was facing him, aged eight, with brown plaits tied with red ribbons, a short floral dress and open sandals. I was holding a recent birthday present— my most prized possession—a brightly painted kaleidoscope. This was my magic portal into a world of brilliant colors and weird and wonderful ever-changing shapes.

I had arrived an hour or so earlier with my mother, father and three-year-old sister Avril. It was "Visit the family in Edgware day." We had traveled across London by bus and underground train from our Sharon Gardens home in East London to our relations who lived in this North London suburb. First, we had a tasty lunch prepared by my Aunts Betty and Eunice at their Franklyn Garden home. Then, we all walked around the corner to

Harrowes Meade to see my Aunt Sally, Uncle Phil and cousins Clive and two-year-old Nigel.

Tea, as usual, had been a delight. My Aunt Sally had a flair for traditional Jewish cooking and her cakes were a local legend. She wrote a cookery column for the Edgware Mizrachi Society and was later to publish "Sally Simons Kosher Cookery Book." She, like my lovely mother, and, in fact most Jewish mothers, believed that food and family gatherings around the kitchen table was the glue that kept Jewish families together and so they cooked constantly with love and pleasure. We had enjoyed a delicious variety of cakes, Cherry Madeira, Coffee Almond and Chocolate Cake with Butter Icing. Then there were the pastries and crunchy cookies. All washed down with strong English afternoon tea served from a big brown betty teapot. Just thinking of this sweet feast made me smile.

"Let me see that," Clive demanded, interrupting my thoughts. He pointed to my kaleidoscope. "How does it work?"

"Here you are," I said showing him how to hold and turn the tube to make the shapes dance.

"If you give it to me, I'll let you see it. It's much better than this. There are people singing and dancing and lots of music and quiz game shows."

The 'it' was the new television that had recently arrived at Harrowes Meade. The year was 1952 and televisions were all the new rage in the United Kingdom, but very few people actually had one.

"Let me see it first," I said.

"Follow me," commanded Clive. We crept down the stairs and Clive quietly opened the lounge door and there it was, in splendid isolation, a small grey box on legs with a nine-inch screen.

"I'll turn it on for you to see, but first you have to give me the kaleidoscope."

I stood there uncertainly, rubbing one leg against the other. I really wanted to see how the television worked, but did I really want to give him my treasured kaleidoscope?

"You can hold it while we watch the television," I said, attempting to bargain.

"No! I want it," he answered, closing the lounge door and heading back up the stairs.

I was conflicted. My kaleidoscope was such special magic. But how would I ever get to see a television program if I didn't give it to him?

In a flash, I had the answer. "Okay. Clive," I said in a loud voice. "You can have it."

Then quietly under my breath with both sets of fingers firmly crossed behind my back. I added, "but only for an hour."

"Good," he grinned taking possession of it. "Now, I'll ask my dad to switch it on. Come on, you are going to like this."

With a flicker, the little grey screen came to life and together with Avril and Nigel we all sat on the floor and watched "Bill and Ben The Flowerpot Men," "Andy Pandy" and "Muffin the Mule." This was followed by a lady called "Lucy" who kept falling all over the place and doing funny things.

Time seemed to fly by as we sat entranced by the characters on the screen

All too soon, it was time to go home. My parents came in with our coats and, as we were about to leave, I made a grab for the kaleidoscope. Clive counter grabbed.

"Give it back! It's mine."

"No, it's not."

"You gave it to me," he yelled.

"Only for an hour," I shouted.

"Hey, what's going on," my father intervened. "Why are you fighting?"

"He's got my kaleidoscope."

"She gave it to me," responded my cousin.

"Yes, but only for an hour."

"No, you gave it to me," Clive yelled. "You didn't say, *just for an hour.*"

My father kneeled down and looked at me, "Vivien did you say he could have the kaleidoscope?"

I looked back into his brown eyes. "Yes, but only for an hour, while we watched the television."

"No, she didn't," interrupted Clive.

My father looked at me again and asked gently. "Did he hear you say, *just for an hour?*"

I bit my tongue and hung my head. *How could I lie to my beloved dad?*

"No. He didn't. I said it under my breath."
My father looked at me wisely. "Then you must give it to him. You must keep your word. Come on now, we'll find you another one."

We said our goodbyes and left with my father carrying my sister and me holding my mother's hand with tears running down my cheeks. I had given away my precious kaleidoscope–my carnival of dreams–just to look at a silly television for a few hours. I wanted it back.

Fast-forward some twenty-five years. I am sitting around a family dining table in Kiryat Arba on the outskirts of Hebron. Clive is now Chaim, a rabbi sporting a thick black bushy beard on his once rosy cheeks. He has seven children aged from one to twelve. We have just finished a delicious and tasty meal cooked by his wife, Dina. My Aunt Sally has now moved from Edgware to Kiryat Arba, and lives in a granny flat next door. My mother and father are visiting from London. It's been a relaxing and enjoyable family get-together in August 1977, celebrating a shared birthday, mine and that of his eldest daughter Ayelet.

In the intervening years, my life has been full of color, excitement and travel. At present, I am working as an interior decorating advisor and salesperson for Danish Interiors in Jerusalem, helping people to decorate their homes with a medley of well designed furniture and dramatically patterned fabrics and rugs.

With lunch over, the children seemed excited about something and suddenly disappeared, only to reappear a few minutes later, with two of them carrying a very large box plainly wrapped in brown paper and string. They plonked it on the table in front of me.

"What's this?"
"Happy birthday Vivvy," they all yelled.
"Open it, open it" said Miri the six-year-old.

I stood up to cut the string and wrapping paper and opened it only to find myself looking at another brown wrapped box which had the children laughing in glee.

"Open it, open it," they all chorused and so it went on, with box after box appearing to peals of childish laughter. Then suddenly a smaller box appeared decoratively wrapped with a ribbon. There was a surprising silence as I ripped off the wrapping and looked inside. There, lying on a bed of tissue, was a kaleidoscope.

My kaleidoscope?

I looked quizzically at Chaim. "Is it...?" I started to ask.

Chaim laughed, shook his head and looked a little embarrassed. "No, I don't know what happened to that one, but over the years I've always felt ashamed about making you give me your kaleidoscope just to let you look at that silly television. So the children suggested I get you a new one and here it is. I'm really sorry about the other one. Am I forgiven?"

I grinned and said. "Of course you are," and picked up the kaleidoscope and held it up to look through it. As the colors swirled and danced into a medley of different shapes. The years slipped away and I was briefly a child again.

"Can we look? Can we look?" came a chorus of voices.

I handed it to them.

"Cool" said Hadassah, the ten-year-old.

It passed from hand to hand.

"Lovely colors" said Rachel, the four-year-old.

I bent down and looked at her. "Would you like this magic kaleidoscope of colors?" I asked her gently.

She held it tightly in her hand, "Yes, please Vivvy."

"It's yours then," I said. "Look after it."

The colors of my life were indeed now as brilliant as those of the kaleidoscope. It was time to hand on the magic and dreams.

A Million Miles from Hollywood

Our Hackney youth club in London's East End was ordinary. There was no other way to describe it. Just plain ordinary.

It was well-used, well-scrubbed and somewhat shabby and was located in the basement of our Brenthouse Road Synagogue. With a table tennis table tucked away in one corner, a well-worn stand up piano in the other, rooms with sliding doors used for classes and a central space with a stage for communal social events. That was it.

Nothing exciting ever happened here. It was a million miles from the magic of Hollywood.

Yet, in the summer of 1959, rumors began to circulate that something exciting and out of the ordinary was about to take place.

Of course, we had heard such stories before; they usually began around late summer to encourage reluctant participants to join in club activities.

However, this time something felt different. Teams of people were seen attempting to bring some color to this rather dismal space. Fresh paint was slapped on flaking walls, dusty curtains were taken down and washed and a pile of folding chairs suddenly grew higher. Something was definitely in the air. But what?

Awards Day was drawing close. This was a Sunday at the end of summer, when pupils, who had excelled in their Hebrew studies, received certificates and those, who were not sport activity challenged, received their sports Oscars: silver plated trophy cups.

Thus, on a sunny Sunday afternoon in early September, there was an audience of some 200 children and parents, sitting in the now pale blue painted, flower-bedecked, revived community hall.

On the stage, behind a row of chairs, a volunteer thumped on the piano accompanied by three discordant recorders, an off key guitar and an enthusiastically loud drummer. Club officials kept rushing in and out, looking anxiously down the street.

Rumors had been flying all week that a Hollywood star was going to be presenting the prizes this year.

"I bet it will be a Mickey Mouse look alike," said Michael, a cynical fourteen-year-old.

"Or Popeye the sailor man," added Linda.

"Absolutely," agreed David. "What film star would want to come here?"

Five minutes stretched into ten and then twenty. Thirty minutes passed and nothing was happening. People were beginning to get restless and starting to complain.

Suddenly, there was the sound of activity outside, a flurry of sound, somebody shouting. "Hold it just there," followed by the sound of cameras clicking.

Then what appeared to be the scent of stardom started to waft into the now quiet and expectant hall, an aura of excitement began to build.

Somebody had arrived. But who was it?

Had our sorry little excuse of a club actually managed to pull off a "famous visitor" to give away this year's prizes?

Heads turned, necks were craned, and all eyes focused on the closed double doors.

Then, with a flourish, as our amateur band came to a noisy crescendo and attempted a ragged fanfare, the doors were flung open.

Was this for real?

There, standing framed in the doorway, with blond hair, red lips, tight dress, uplifted breasts and a white mink cape was the Hollywood star, Jayne Mansfield. Her husband Mickey Hargitay, the former Mr. Universe, stood behind her with rippling muscles bulging under his jacket.

There was a stunned silence and mouths fell open in astonishment as club officials led the way to the stage. Jayne followed, swaying between the chairs, smiling as she walked. In procession behind her were Mickey, the Mayor of Hackney and various other officials.

Once the visitors were on stage, an enormous bunch of roses suddenly appeared and were presented to the star. She accepted them graciously and sat down as did the other visitors. Then the Club President stood up and announced with a flourish, "Ladies and Gentlemen, boys and girls I am proud to introduce today a famous film star, direct from Hollywood, who is here to present this year's prizes, Jayne Mansfield."

There was a roar of approval, as the audience clapped enthusiastically in response.

She stood up waiting for the applause to stop and smiling replied, "Thank you very much. I am really happy to be here in England in this beautiful country, working on my new film, 'Too Hot To Handle.' Mickey and I are really honored to be invited to present the prizes in your lovely club on this special day."

She sat down again to more applause and a few wolf whistles, as the band attempted another tune, and the club dance group demonstrated its ever developing ragged movement skills.

Then it was time for her to present the prizes. First, the studious Hebrew students marched onto the stage to receive their certificates, encouraged by proud clapping parents. Then it was "Big Cup Time" the awards ceremony for the table tennis champion and the football and athletic stars.

To loud applause, three confident fifteen-year-olds, marched onto the stage with their slicked back hair, well-scrubbed cheeks and white shirts.

Jayne shook their hands, handed them their trophy cups and said a few words to each of them. Then she did something extraordinary: she bent down and planted a big red kiss on each of the three champions' cheeks.

For a moment, the boys looked startled and embarrassed, but then they straightened up, smirked and walked off the stage with a swagger, each with bright red lips imprinted on their cheeks.

The audience roared its approval, clapping enthusiastically. Then the officials started to move off the stage with Jayne and her husband in the lead. There was a buzz of noise, a whirl of flashing cameras and, in an instant, she was gone and Brenthouse Road Youth Club was back to its normal ordinary self.

Had she actually been here?

Well, yes. The evidence was right there before our eyes.

For some time, three pairs of bright red lips were showcased on the faces of three boys who, not wanting to damage their badges of honor, managed to avoid washing that side of their faces for several weeks.

That bizarre memory suddenly flashed before my eyes as I stood in a crowd of people patiently waiting in a line that snaked its way around the YMCA block and then back again along the Embarcadero. It was January 2011 and I was now living in beautiful San Francisco. The poster for the open casting for film extras for a new action thriller about to start shooting in the city had specified, "all shapes and sizes," and they were certainly well represented here. I was towards the end of this crowd of straggly hopefuls, all drawn by the still strangely powerful Hollywood dream.

As we waited in line, to hand in our photos and our hopes, I suspected that though I was now physically closer to Hollywood, in reality I was just as far away as that star struck fifteen-year-old all those years ago in London, watching the magic of a star performance for a few brief moments.

My Five Minutes of Fame

*W*hat was I doing on the front page of a national newspaper sandwiched between the English Prime Minister Harold Macmillan and the top-hatted student president of Sussex University's Antiquarian Society?

Breakfast was nearly over as I quietly took my place in the students' dining room. It had been a late night partying with friends and I was looking forward to a gentle start to the day.

Whoosh. Suddenly something whizzed across the room and landed on the table in front of me nearly knocking over my mug of tea. It was a rolled up newspaper which slowly unfurled itself to reveal a smiling face.

Whatever was going on?

In front of me was the daily edition of "The Daily Mail," one of England's major newspapers. It was Wednesday, June 12, 1963 and I was nineteen, a first year student at the newly established University of Sussex. The smiling face looked vaguely familiar, the eyes strikingly similar to mine.

"Wait a minute," I muttered to myself. "That's me."

79

The events of the previous day, Tuesday, June 11, 1963 came rushing back. It had been a day of pomp and ceremony with the installation of Viscount Monckton as the first Chancellor of the new University of Sussex.

The ceremony had taken place off campus as Basil Spence's unique and interesting buildings nestling in the Sussex Downs were still taking shape. The site selected for the ceremony was Brighton's Dome, a part of the fanciful and exotic Royal Pavilion Estate. This provided a fitting stage for the swirl of colorful academic gowns and famous faces participating from around the world: Paul Henri Spaak, Belgian Foreign Minister, George Woodcock TUC General Secretary, Lady Violet Bonham-Carter, Basil Spence, Asa Briggs and John Fulton to name but a few.

However, all attention was focused on Prime Minister Harold Macmillan who was attending to receive the Honorary Degree of Doctor of Laws. His much anticipated acceptance speech was to be his first public statement since the resignation of his Secretary of State for War, John Profumo.

The Profumo case had exploded in the press a few days earlier when the minister had admitted lying to the House of Commons when he previously denied any impropriety with Christine Keeler. The Prime Minister had responded by going to Buckingham Palace to report to the Queen on the growing crisis and security implications of the affair. He had also summoned his cabinet for a crisis cabinet meeting for today, June 12 with ministers being told to cancel engagements, both at home and abroad.

Yet on June 11, 1963, amidst this political furor, attempting to show that business was continuing as normal, he had decided to keep his long-standing commitment to come to the University of Sussex, for the installation of its first Chancellor.

The press loved it. Hordes of journalists, both national and international, had descended on Brighton and were following his every move and word. They missed nothing, recording his acknowledgement of the gathered crowds, his smile to the woman who called "Good Luck Sir" and his pointed ignoring of the group of heckling students, one of whom shouted, "You'll need it."

In his speech of thanks for his honorary degree of Doctor of Laws from Sussex, Macmillan only made one oblique reference to the political turmoil he faced as Prime Minister. In response to the tribute to his career read by Pro-Vice Chancellor Professor Asa Briggs he said, "I thought the story was tersely and factually unfolded, a story of ups and downs." Pausing slightly, he continued with a smile, "but everything came right in the end. Of course, one has to try to keep it right."

He concluded by alluding to an incident involving the suspension of seven students for ignoring university curfew regulations. His statement, "the fewer rules the better," was met by laughter and applause from the audience.

Then the formal ceremony was over and the guests headed out to the campus for lunch in the university. This was where, later in the afternoon, our paths were to cross.

It was around 3:00 p.m. and I was standing chatting with friends in the quadrangle of Falmer House, one of the two completed buildings on the new campus and its social hub. The water in the moat rippled gently in the sunlight reflecting the distinctive soft pink bricks of the building. We were still wearing our undergraduate gowns, just hanging around waiting for something to happen.

Suddenly, my friend Sheila (who by a strange coincidence, was the niece of Iain Mcleod, a member of Macmillan's government) pointed to some students grouped in the middle of the quad.

"Look. Let's go and see what's happening over there."

"Is that the Prime Minister standing there among the top hats and bowlers of the Antiquarian Society?"

"Yes, I think it is."

"That's curious. I heard a rumor that Bob Hine was one of the students heckling Macmillan yesterday outside St Peter's Church, at the university dedication service. What's he doing laughing and joking with him now? A bit hypocritical don't you think?"

"Well, he is obviously practicing to be a politician," said Sheila with a grin. "Let's get closer and see what's going on."

As we joined the crowd, there was a sudden movement, and the Prime Minister reached up his hand and playfully tipped the top hat over Bob Hine's eyes. The Press went mad and the world exploded in the light of flashing cameras. A moment of mirth in the midst of a serious political drama.

Bob, in response to the Prime Minister's action, officially declared that Macmillan was now "A Genuine Antiquarian."

Wallop. My reflections on the previous days events were rudely interrupted. I was being pelted from all directions with rolled up newspapers, accompanied by the chant "You're famous! You're famous!"

The "Daily Mail," "Daily Sketch," "Daily Telegraph and Morning Post" all bounced on the table, unfurling to reveal me grinning, sandwiched between the Prime Minister and Bob Hine. Then, there it was, the grand old lady of newspapers itself: "The Times." I had actually made the back page with a full-length photo standing alongside another photo, titled "Tension at Tuscaloosa," a reminder of the crisis in Alabama where President Kennedy had just sent in troops to force the admission of two black students at the University of Alabama.

Today, indeed, I was to have my five minutes of fame. I was, *The Laughing Girl,* as Reuters referred to me when my father contacted them for a copy of the main photograph. I might as well enjoy it while it lasted.

Tomorrow I would be the newspaper wrapping for fish and chips from Brighton's local fish and chip shop.

The Lecture

Coffee was being served to our distinguished guest at the end of dinner as the sun began to set over the green rolling Sussex Downs. It cast a warm golden glow over the oak tables and chairs of the university refectory. I stood up and made my excuses, saying that I would return in five minutes.

As secretary of Sussex University's History Society, it was my responsibility to check that everything was in order in the debating chamber where our guest speaker was about to deliver his much-anticipated lecture.

I quickly made my way through the open plan common rooms with their brightly cushioned Scandinavian easy chairs and entered a strangely silent debating chamber. *Where was the usual noisy student laughter and banter?*

The room on that early evening in November, 1963, was full; row upon row of students sat on the circular pine sunken amphitheatre style seats, looking serious-not a word was being uttered—and an uncanny and unnerving silence permeated the usually noisy room. *What was wrong?*

As I looked around trying to understand what had happened, I caught the eye of my friend Jenny. She urgently beckoned me over. *Could she cast some light on this unexpectedly bizarre gathering?*

As I drew closer, Jenny did not greet me with her usual smile, but was looking really upset.

"Isn't the news terrible?" she said in a quiet voice.

"What's terrible? What's happened?"

"You haven't heard?"

"Heard what? I've been in the refectory entertaining our speaker for the last hour or so."

Her reply came like a bolt out of the blue.

"President Kennedy's been shot."

"Where? When? How do you know?"

My questions ran into each other as the shock of her news sunk in and I tried to understand this devastating event.

"A group of us were relaxing in the student bar downstairs watching the news when it was announced as "breaking news." It apparently had just happened in Dallas, Texas."

"Is he going to be alright?"

"No. He didn't survive. Johnson's been sworn in as President."

I stood there in the quiet crowded debating chamber, shocked into silence, completely forgetting that I was expected back in the refectory to collect our guest speaker.

"What about the lecture? Is it still going to take place?" asked Jenny.

Her question jolted me back into the present with a start.

"I don't know. Let me go and find out."

I rushed out of the debating chamber, running through the student lounge and back to the refectory, where our guest and other members of the history society were waiting for my return.

"Are we ready to start?" asked John, the History Society president. He suddenly stopped, "Are you okay? Vivien, you look very pale!"

I stood there, confused and uncertain, not knowing what to say, and then I just blurted it out, "I've just heard the most terrible news. President Kennedy has been assassinated."

There was a stunned silence.

"Are you sure?" asked our distinguished guest in a shaken voice.

As he asked the question, I suddenly realized what I had done. Sir Isaiah Berlin was a personal friend of President Kennedy, and a frequent visitor to The White House and I had just announced this shocking news without so much as a warning of what I was about to say.

"Yes, I am afraid so. I've just been told it was announced on the news."

"Would you excuse me for a few moments?" said Sir Isaiah in a very quiet voice.

He slowly walked away from us towards the huge windows at the far end of the refectory, standing silently with his back to us, staring at the twilight lit countryside.

"What shall we do? Cancel the lecture?" I asked.

"Let's see what Sir Isaiah wants to do," replied John.

This seemed to be the general consensus so we all sat down again and silently waited. After about ten minutes, Sir Isaiah Berlin turned around and slowly came back to where we were waiting.

"Would you like us to cancel the lecture?" asked John.

"No, let's not keep the students waiting any longer. Lead the way."

He followed us into the packed lecture hall and strode onto the central platform where John briefly introduced him. Then, without commenting on the news or referring to it in any way, he gave his scheduled lecture on, of all subjects, Machiavelli.

The Queen's Visit

A light drizzle was falling, as the students started to gather in the open courtyard of Sussex University between the student building and the library. They stood chatting in groups, with duffle coats buttoned up against the cold and damp. It was not the weather the university authorities had hoped for when they planned this special occasion for November 13, 1964.

Peter was standing at the junction where the path from Falmer House joined the more imposing walkway leading up to the steps of the library. At last, the much-anticipated day had arrived; HM Queen Elizabeth II was coming to officially open the newly completed library building.

He pulled up the hood of his navy duffle coat as the drizzle, with no respect for the occasion, turned to rain and large drops started plopping onto the path in steady rhythm. He stared fascinated as a path-side puddle soaked the grass verge and slowly started to bubble up and spread onto the main path. A sudden cheer and cries of welcome brought him back to the present.

Looking up, he saw the royal party approaching with the queen holding a huge umbrella. She was wearing a warm brown wool coat with fur trimming and a round fur hat, black court shoes, and her signature black leather handbag on her left arm.

She had almost reached the spot where he was standing and, when looking down, he realized in horror that the puddle on the path had grown to a small pond. From the recesses of his memory, an image flashed to mind of one of his favorite boyhood stories and, without pausing to think, he pulled off his coat. Then, with a Sir Walter Raleigh flourish, he went into a deep bow throwing his coat down, cloak-like across the pool of water at the feet of the queen. She stopped, startled for a moment, then turned and smiled her thanks to him. Then, she navigated her way around the coat and the water, careful not to walk on his coat, and continued up the steps and into the library. Press cameras flashed, recording the incident for the evening newspapers.

Inside the library, students were sitting at the study cubicles. Debby had arrived early, as she had been out partying the night before and had not finished the essay that she was due to present at a tutorial in a couple of hours. She had wedged her chair under the desk determined to focus on the work at hand.

Meanwhile, the vice-chancellor was guiding the royal party through the book-lined library. His assistant was going along a parallel path, quietly motioning the students to rise and acknowledge the queen's presence. The royal party made slow progress with the queen occasionally stopping to speak to a student.

As the queen approached the row where Debby was working, everyone stood up at the expected signal, except for Debby. She couldn't move; she was stuck with her chair jammed under the desk. Panic stricken, aware of a frantically gesturing assistant and fellow students hissing out of the side of their mouths, "Stand Up! Stand Up!" she couldn't and the more she struggled, the more she was stuck.

As the queen swept by, not indicating anything was amiss, she hung her head in shame. Visions of being dragged off and locked in the Tower of London flashed. *Was she the first person in history not to have risen as her monarch approached?* There was silence. No one said a word.

However, fortunately for Debby and her place in history, no press cameras had been close by to record the embarrassing incident.

Ballad of an Apple

Part 1.

She shuffled into the Office
To pay her council rent,
A shabby owlish figure
Pathetically small and bent.

With walking stick in hand,
And whiskers on her chin,
Her carefully counted rent
Was clutched in fingers thin.

She plonked it on the counter,
"It's me Ted," she did say
"He's been again and wants to take
All my furniture away."

Ted, the counter, placidly sipped
His ten thirty-office brew,
And entered once again,
Her two pounds three and two.

"You and your council flat are safe,
So don't you worry dear,"
Murmured he the reassuring phrase,
"We'll not let your brother near."

Her owlish eyes regarded him,
From behind NHS frame,
Seeing once more a security
In words and face the same.

Vivien Zielin

"I hear you are off to convalesce,
Now everything will be fine,
Just you go enjoy yourself
In Clacton's lovely sunshine."

She turned to go, and turned again,
Saying with lonely smile,
"I'll bring you back some Clacton rock,
But here's something else meanwhile."

She handed him an apple,
From a "Buy from Ben," brown bag,
"I'll eat it later," Ted did say,
Stubbing out his fag.

She shambled out of the office,
By the next tenant the clerk was faced,
On the shelf behind the switchboard,
The green apple it was placed.

The apple, it was forgotten,
It languished all alone,
On that shelf beneath the office clutter,
Near the ever ringing phone.

And so a month meandered by,
Dunked in office routine,
The apple lost its luster,
Turned a wrinkled, mottled green.

Routine was on the office,
Yet something seemed out of place,
Someone was missing,
A familiar tenant face.

Eyeballing Big Croc

"I wonder where our Mabel is?"
Ted one morn did say,
"She was due back from Clacton
Four weeks ago today."

"It's not like her to miss a rent.
There's something wrong for sure,
She's always in so regular,
Shuffling through that door."

He picked up the telephone,
And dialed the Welfare Board,
To find out if she was ill,
And if somebody had called.

The Welfare Board, they grew concerned,
No word at all, had they,
They'd phone the convalescent home,
To see if she was okay.

From Clacton now, there was no news,
She'd not been there at all,
So all the local hospitals,
The Board began to call.

The Housing Manager entered,
Most perturbed was he,
"The caretaker will have to break in,
And see what he can see."

Part 2.

I lifted up the papers,
And lying there behind,
An apple mottled and flabby,
A suddenly frightening find.

It's decay assumed a character,
A calendar of days,
A tangibly horrifying reminder
Of people's neglectful ways.

And so it sat there on the shelf,
A terrifying image for me,
Until a rent collector,
He ate it for his tea.

Note.
This poem is dedicated to the memory of a woman whose name I was too upset to remember in the summer of 1966.
NHS is National Health Service.
Clacton an English seaside town.
Rock is sugar candy.
Fag is slang for cigarette.

The Man with a Table Leg

Jack pushed open the door of his local pub. His throat felt dry and dusty and he could hardly wait for that first cooling sip of beer to quench his raging thirst. He was a carpenter by trade and had spent that hot summer's day in September, 1999, working on the renovation of a dilapidated Victorian house down by the canal. He was carrying a long package, wrapped in a paint-splattered sheet under his arm.

His two drinking partners Tom and Mike, were sitting at the polished wooden bar waiting for him. They had been friends for years, from the time they had done their national army service together in the late 1950's. Meeting around 6:00 p.m. for a relaxing beer and smoke was a weekday working ritual.

"Pint of bitter," Jack said to Bill the Bartender, as he slid onto the barstool. He carefully propped the sheet-covered package he was carrying up against the side of the bar.

"What's that you've got there? asked Tom, "Your old army rifle?"

Jack grinned, "Don't be daft. It's this old carved table leg I found in the attic of the Victorian. I thought it might come in handy one day. Better than tossing it in the skip."

Jack glanced round the pub. It was almost empty with just one couple talking earnestly in an alcove and a few men clustered around the billiards table. As they sat and chatted, the pub began to fill up. It had been a hot day and people were thirsty.

Jack was on his second beer when Tom suggested a game of darts.

"We've just got time for a game before the replay of the highlights of yesterday's Arsenal football match."

The darts game finished with Mike, as usual, scoring highest and they settled back at the bar to watch the television replay of yesterday's football match. The evening passed pleasantly and the pub filled up with more people becoming noisier and smokier. As Arsenal supporters, the friends thought it only right to celebrate each of their five goals, with another round of beer. It was now 8:30 p.m.

"I'd better be going," said Jack. "Doreen will have my supper waiting."

He pushed himself off the stool, a trifle unsteadily, and started walking towards the door. He had had more beers than usual on an empty stomach and didn't feel too steady on his feet.

"Hey Jack! Don't forget your package," Mike yelled after him.

Several people in the pub looked up and then down again quickly as Jack stumbled back to the bar to take his sheet-wrapped package.

"Thanks mate. See you both tomorrow," he said as he left.

It was now dark with a sliver of a moon as Jack made his way down Victoria Park Road. The formerly grand Victorian mansions were set back from the road and the oak trees in their front gardens cast dark shadows onto the street. The street was deserted and he found himself weaving from side to side on the sidewalk, humming, "We all live in a yellow submarine." Doreen his wife had promised him lamb chops for dinner and he was looking forward to them, but he was much later than arranged and had definitely had too much to drink. He'd have to make it up to her tomorrow. In the distance, he could hear the wailing siren of a police car.

The police call went out at 8:35 p.m. "Urgent! All units in Hackney area proceed immediately to Victoria Park Road. There has been a report of a suspicious man in the area carrying a gun. Proceed with caution."

The two policemen on patrol in nearby Hackney Road acknowledged the call first, turned on their siren and sped towards Victoria Park Road. Turning into the road, they stopped the car and got out. The street was deserted and they could see in the distance just one person meandering down the road carrying a long menacing package.

The two policemen quickly moved to the boot of the car and unlocked it, taking out two bulletproof vests and two Glock pistols. They belonged to a new breed of British policemen, trained and armed for emergency situations like this. They were pumped up and ready to go.

As Jack neared the bottom of the road close to his home, he suddenly noticed two dark figures looming in front of him.

"Stop! Armed Police! Put down your gun and get down on the ground!" they shouted.

Who were they talking to? Was there somebody behind him? Jack wondered, as he started to turn round to look, but was stopped by an even louder shout.

"Stop! Armed Police! Drop the gun and don't move!"

Did they mean him? They were mistaken. He didn't have a gun.

"But I haven't got a gun," he said, "Look, it's only a wooden table leg."

As he clumsily moved his arm to show them their mistake, the shot rang out, hitting him in the chest and spinning him round. He fell to the ground still clutching the table leg, a look of surprise on his face.

The two policemen moved cautiously towards him with pistols drawn. The younger of the two, drew closer to Jack lying motionless on the sidewalk. He bent towards the package and kicked it away from Jack's body.

"It looks like some sort of rifle," he started to say, and then stopped in horror.

The sheet had slid off the package suddenly revealing an ornately carved wooden table leg.

"Oh no!" he screamed, "It's not a gun. It's just an old table leg. Who said it was a gun?"

A crescendo of police and ambulance sirens roared to the spot as Jack lay sprawled silently on the sidewalk next to the bollard that was to bear witness, as a flower garlanded memorial to him for many years to come.

The Chicken or The Blouse?

"I want to speak to a manager," said the man shuffling up to the customer service counter in the food department of the chain store.

"Can I help you?" asked the assistant.

"No, I want to speak to a manager," repeated the man holding a plastic bag with the store's logo. He was a slight man with an elderly stoop and strands of grey hair stretched across his balding head. He was dressed in a shabby tweed jacket, crumpled brown trousers and a paisley tie showing signs of an earlier meal. There was an air of vulnerability about him.

"Just a minute and I'll find somebody to help you," the women answered, picking up a phone. Her voice boomed out over the loudspeaker system, "Manager needed in the food department."

The young man who appeared a few minutes later wore a Marks and Spencer navy suit, blue-striped shirt and highly polished black shoes.

"Hello, my name is John Davies. I'm the manager of the food department. How can I help you?"

"Well it's about the barbecued chicken I bought over the weekend. There's something wrong with it," the man said, handing the manager the plastic bag.

"What's the matter with the chicken?"

"Well, it's a bit difficult to explain, but there is something not quite right about it, a strange taste and smell."

"Well let's have a look at it," said the manager putting his hand in the bag to take out the chicken. He looked puzzled, as his hand reappeared holding a bundle of bones.

"Where's the chicken you are complaining about? I need to see the chicken, not just the bones," he said with some distaste, squirting some hand sanitizer from a nearby dispenser.

The elderly man looked up with a nervous smile and confided, "At first, when I started my meal, the chicken seemed okay, but then it started to taste a bit funny so I thought I had imagined it. I tried a bit more, but it still seemed somewhat strange so I continued to eat a bit more to see if I could find out why it didn't taste like it usually did. And then it was gone before I could solve the mystery. But there was definitely something not right with it so I thought I must bring it back and ask for a replacement."

The manager looked a trifle perplexed. Here was this elderly man bringing him a bag of bones with the store's receipt and a story about it tasting strange.

What should he do? His not-so-distant training had focused on a manager taking decisive action and giving the customer the benefit of the doubt. Besides, the guy looked like he was in need of several good meals. It was a no-brainer!

"Very well sir," he said, "I'll get you a replacement chicken from the barbecue and I'm sorry you were not satisfied with us. We'll have to try harder next time."

"Thank you," the man said, beaming.

Two months later, in the spring of 1979 at a training session at the department store's head office, the incident was being recounted to a group of trainee managers.

"That event occurred on Holloway Road, one of our North London branches," said the instructor, as she finished telling the story. "This second incident happened in our Oxford Circus West End store. When I finish, we'll take a fifteen-minute coffee break, and then resume for a discussion of the issues raised."

The smartly dressed woman walked up to the counter of the Oxford Circus store. She was wearing a Calvin Klein beige suit and black stilettos.

"I want to return this blouse," she said handing a bag to the nearest supervisor in the fashion department. As the supervisor took the expensive blouse out of the bag, she noticed a small wine stain on one of the sleeves.

"I am returning this blouse," the customer said, "because it has numbers written on the back." The blouse was beige silk with a bright tropical flower design.

"Numbers? Where?" asked the supervisor.

"There," replied the woman pointing to the side of the blouse, "I went nightclubbing last night with friends, and when I was dancing, people kept asking me why my blouse had numbers all down one side."

The supervisor examined the blouse and then held it up to the light. "There are no numbers here," she stated. "Were you and your friends drinking in the club?"

"Yes, of course. We all shared a bottle of wine, but that has nothing to do with it. Everyone saw the numbers glowing when I was dancing. I want my money back."

"A fine old story," thought the supervisor. "She's stained the sleeve with wine and has concocted some ridiculous story so she can get a refund."

Turning to face the customer she said, "I'm sorry, but this blouse is stained. I cannot give you your money back."

The woman was becoming increasingly irate and her voice went up several decibels. Other customers shopping in the vicinity turned to look towards the commotion.

"I tell you this blouse has numbers written on it. I demand that you give me a refund."

"I am sorry madam, but I cannot, at this stage, authorize a refund. However, I am prepared to send the blouse to our head office for testing—to see if there is anything really wrong with it. I'll give you a receipt and somebody will contact you in a few days. I'm afraid that's the best I can do under the circumstances." The customer, still looking annoyed, reluctantly agreed.

"All right, settle down now," said the instructor, following the promised coffee break. "Let's get started. One of these two customers is a con artist. Which one do you think it is? Write your answers on these cards and pass them back to me."

As the cards were handed back to her, the instructor started laughing. "No matter how many times I give this training session, the response is always the same. Every group seems to have the same fixed perceptions based on stereotypes. A pathetic elderly man—how could he be anything but genuine—while a loud flashily dressed woman with damaged goods must be up to something suspicious. Now listen carefully as here, in fact, is the follow up to these two incidents."

The food manger was writing up his daily report. Something had been bothering him all afternoon. He just could not shake the feeling that something was not right. It was those greasy bones. If the chicken had tasted so bad, why would the man eat it and not just return it? It didn't make sense. On an impulse, he picked up the phone and called the nearest branch to his Holloway store. On recounting the incident to that store's manager, there was a sudden laugh as the man exclaimed, "The cunning geezer! He pulled the same trick on me last week. I also gave him another chicken."

That was enough to convince John Davies to contact every one of the chain stores in London. The story was the same in each one. All in all, this pathetic little man had managed to persuade twenty-six stores to give him replacement chickens.

Immediate action was required so a warning poster featuring the "chicken man" was circulated to all the retail chains stores in the region.

Meanwhile, after a battery of tests on the blouse at the head office laboratory, the number mystery was solved. The woman was absolutely right. There was a series of numbers embedded in her blouse. They were manufacturing codes and they were printed on one of the seams of the blouse, and did not show up under normal lighting; they only could only be seen under infrared light.

When the woman was dancing in the club, the dance floor had been illuminated by flashing laser and club LED lighting. Hence, the numbers had magically appeared, only to disappear when she moved away from the dance floor.

"Don't look so surprised," the instructor smiled at the silent and embarrassed group of management trainees, of whom I was one. "Just be aware that nothing is ever as simple or obvious as it appears. So when you are in your stores and a customer approaches you with a complaint, keep an open mind and remember to never ever judge a book by its cover."

A Star of a Street

I looked up into a pair of amazing blue eyes as recognition dawned. The box of Waterford crystal glasses that I had just carefully wrapped, halted mid air in my startled hand as I bit my tongue to stop myself from blurting out, "You're.... aren't you?"

After all, that was not how one behaved in Beauchamp Place.

It was the early eighties and Beauchamp Place was an exotic street, tucked away just a few turnings from Harrods and somewhat hidden from the humdrum of the rest of Knightsbridge. With its Georgian fronted buildings, designer boutiques and bijoux restaurants, it was both edgy and fashionable and was the stomping ground for those stars looking for something just a little different.

The place where I worked was certainly different. In fact, it was regarded as a total outsider, both loved and hated by the rest of the Beauchamp Place merchants. Loved because it was popular and successful and attracted visitors from around the world. Hated because it brought down the tone of the neighborhood and it was

Eyeballing Big Croc

generally agreed that it most certainly did not belong there. Called "The Reject China Shop," it had originally been the brainchild of David Queensberry. He had decided to sell "not quite perfect pieces of china," from companies such as Royal Doulton, Wedgwood, Royal Worcester and Spode and make them available at affordable prices to his aristocratic, but often impoverished friends and acquaintances. He had been welcomed with open arms; after all, he was "The 12th Marquess of Queensberry." However, with his design background, he soon moved on to develop his other interests and become one of the leading ceramicists in the United Kingdom.

The shop was then acquired by the present owner, a gung-ho buccaneering businessman who, every morning incensed his neighboring retailers anew, by unpacking all the new china and glass deliveries slap bang in the middle of the pavement. Crates, packing materials and cartons would be piled up as new goods were crammed onto crowded shelves. Only when everything was unpacked, would the warehouseman load everything still remaining on the pavement onto a trolley and move it around the corner to a nearby mews garage that served as a warehouse. The shop, spread across three of the Georgian buildings was, however, very successful as was verified by the constant stream of customers from all over the world seeking affordable quality china and crystal.

"Excuse me, can I please have my bill?"

The man patiently standing in front of me was of a slight build around five feet eight with short silver curly hair and a well-weathered tan skin. I struggled to stop myself from sinking into the compelling liquid pools of his beautiful blue eyes, staring, without being aware of it, at my hero, Paul Newman, actually standing in touching distance of me in front of the counter. A woman, whom I had noticed standing silently to one side, started to smile and I realized that it was his wife, the actress Joanna Woodward and that she had actually been waiting for this expected reaction from me, obviously a regular occurrence.

As I handed him the bag of boxed crystal and completed the transaction, he gave me a friendly grin accepting the star-struck recognition that obviously accompanied him on every public outing with casual nonchalance. His wife turned and gave me a friendly smile as she took his arm and they walked together down the steps and out onto Beauchamp Place.

Among the many regular visitors to the store at this time was Larry Hagman, famous as the scheming J.R. Ewing in the popular series, "Dallas." He used to sweep into the store with magnetic presence, relishing his fame and obviously enjoying it, as customers flocked to ask for his autograph. To each and every one, he would respond by handing out a Monopoly-style dollar bill with a photograph of him on one side and the words "Not worth the paper it's printed on" on the other. His fans loved it.

From the rival television series "Dynasty," Joan Collins made regular appearances, often staying in character as the deliciously bitchy Alexis Carrington.

"Do you have any decanter labels?" she asked me on one occasion.

"Yes," I replied. "We have ceramic labels for brandy, whisky, gin and bourbon."

"That's not how you pronounce 'bourbon,' she said with some distain, completely ignoring my embarrassment. "It's not the French royal family. It's pronounced 'Burrbon'."

I must admit that I indulged in some quiet satisfaction later that day, when her then husband Ron Kass came into the shop and said, "Don't bother to hurry dear, they have just towed the Rolls."

"Serves you right, you bitch," I thought somewhat uncharitably.

The Beauchamp Place traffic wardens were characters in themselves and they provided hours of entertainment. This particular group of enforcers never touched the smaller cars. Nothing less than a Ferrari, Porsche, Lamborghini, Mercedes or Rolls Royce would do for them. You could see their obvious glee as they fixed the chains around these expensive executive toys and lifted them into the backs of their trucks and then hauled them off to the car pounds on the other side of London. It would take hours for their owners to get them released.

On one occasion, however, they did not touch a large black Mercedes which appeared on the street around noon. It was wrapped like a present with a huge red ribbon topped by a gigantic red bow. It attracted quite an audience as passersby stopped to see what was going on. After an hour or so, three men and a woman in business suits came out of the nearby San Lorenzo restaurant and approached the car.

The woman produced a bunch of keys and casually slid them across the roof of the Mercedes to one of the men saying, "Here you are James. This is your prize for being "top financial advisor of the year."

"Cool, "James replied nonchalantly. "Thanks."

Looking very pleased with himself, he proceeded to tug at the bow and unlock the car door. The four of them got in and drove off with James sporting a wide satisfied beam. The red ribbon shimmied down into the gutter and was forgotten.

"It's alright for some," a voice was heard to say as everyone else continued on their way.

However, the true star of the street was not from the movie world, but from the world of royalty. Diana, Princess of Wales would often be spotted shopping incognito following a visit to one of her favorite restaurants either Ménage a Trois, which served only starters and desserts or San Lorenzo.

"I'm looking for a present for my daughter," said the visitor from Texas as he walked into the section of the store I was managing one morning. "It's her birthday next week. She will be twelve years old and I want to take her something really special when I go home to Dallas next Tuesday."

I knew immediately what he was looking for as I said, "I think she will like this."

I reached up to the top shelf and carefully lifted down a beautifully boxed Royal Doulton-Nisbet, limited edition doll of Diana, Princess of Wales in her wedding gown. With a delicate porcelain face and flowing gown, it was indeed a present to treasure.

"This is lovely," he said smiling. "It's just perfect. I'll take it."

As I finished packing it safely, a movement caught my eye through the window.

Immediately opposite, on the other side of the street, one of Princess Diana's favorite designers, Bruce Oldfield, had recently opened a boutique and in its early days she used to come and go virtually unnoticed accompanied by just a single bodyguard. I had just spotted her leaving the boutique, rosy-cheeked and relaxed with her head slightly down.

"While you are looking at the doll for your daughter," I said pointing to the window, "the real Princess Diana is actually standing over there."

He rushed to the window to look.

"Oh, isn't she lovely? So natural," he said as he watched, entranced. "Now that's really something to tell my daughter about when I get home. Thank you so much."

He left the shop beaming, clutching the boxed Princess Diana doll to his chest as he watched the real princess walk down the steps, get into her car and drive away down that fascinating hodgepodge of a street that was Beauchamp Place.

The China Ware House Company

C^{*rash*!}

I stood in front of my soon-to-be-opened gift shop at 21 Carnaby Street, blinking in the midday sun, my mouth agape in sheer disbelief.

Just a few seconds earlier, right in front of my eyes, somebody had been hurled through the plate glass display window of the shop opposite.

A confrontation between a Mod and a Rocker (a fairly common occurrence between the two groups who gathered each weekend on Carnaby Street) had suddenly escalated into a fight. An angry leather clad rocker had picked up the smaller nifty dressed mouthy mod and literally thrown him through the nearest shop window.

The mod was lying sprawled among the window's contents, surrounded by shards of broken glass, with blood trickling down his forehead and a startled grin transfixed on his face. Fortunately for him, it was a fabric shop which, together with his parka, had protected him from more serious injury. His mates stood on the sidewalk mouthing obscenities. The rockers had disappeared in the commotion and were nowhere to be seen.

The shop owner was jumping up and down on the pavement in fury yelling, "Look what those effing bastards have done to my shop."

In the distance, the sound of barking dogs could be heard as the Saturday afternoon police dog patrol drew close to investigate the noisy incident.

"Hey, what's going on here. Break it up," yelled a policeman holding back a snarling German Shepherd pulling on his leash.

This was Carnaby Street in the mid 1980's, a sad caricature of its once famous cool. Now it was run down, seedy, raw and in your face. These were the streets prowled by the blond crew cut, kilted and man-skirted Jean Paul Gaultier, looking for street cred and outrageous fashion statements to turn into expensive chic for the safer streets of Knightsbridge.

This was no Beauchamp Place. This was something else. Yet this was the very reason I was here. It was the only Central London location available to make my dream of building a gift and dinnerware business from scratch, a reality.

The morning had started ordinarily enough with me sitting in Bambu in nearby Fouberts Court, drinking coffee and chatting with my hairdresser friends, Paul and Kitty.

"What's happening? Why are you and Robert now going to open The China Ware House Company on Carnaby Street?" asked Paul. "I thought you had signed a lease for 12 Ganton Street."

"We have," I replied, "but it's a listed eighteenth century building and the neighboring shop which backs onto it, is in dispute with the landlords and they keep causing problems with the renovations. We were supposed to open in May and now it's already the end of July."

"So where are you putting all the stock, the cups and saucers and teapots and giftware you ordered in Birmingham at the Spring Fair in February?"

"Oh, at the moment, The China Ware House Company is located in my parent's home in Hackney. My mother is having a great time. Whenever there's a knock on the door and a truck driver says, "*Delivery for the China Ware House. Where should I put it?*" she replies, "*Put it here,*" enjoying every moment of seeing her daughter's dream of opening a giftware shop in London's West End become a reality.

"The house must be getting pretty crowded," laughed Paul.

"Yes it is and that's why we had a meeting with the landlords a couple of weeks ago and they agreed to let us have the corner property at 21 Carnaby Street which has just become vacant while they settle the Ganton Street issue."

"But what about the shop fittings?" queried Kitty.

"Now that presents a bit of a challenge, as we can't afford to spend much on temporary premises, but we have found some inexpensive shelves in Habitat and some artist friends are going to paint signs for the shop. Let's hope it stays warm as the shop has no shop front, just metal shutters."

"Where's Robert?" asked Paul. "I haven't seen him for a while."

"Oh, he's in Italy for a long weekend visiting his mother in Turin before we open next week."

Robert was my partner in "The China Ware House Company." A volatile Italian, we worked together as department managers at The Reject China Shop in Beauchamp Place, Knightsbridge and had discovered that we shared a common dream of setting up a giftware and dinnerware shop catering to visitors from around the world. Hence, our need for an affordable Central London location. The Reject China Shop discouraged any personal relationships among its staff and we would have been fired on the spot if it had been known we were actually actively planning to set up a rival business. So we acted as complete strangers on their premises totally ignoring each other. It had taken nine months of searching for premises in our spare time to come up with the Ganton Street property. None of the West End property consultants had been remotely interested in talking with two idealists with very little money and no previous record of shop ownership.

However, what we did have was a lot of chutzpah and we had bluffed our way into the offices of the landlords of the Carnaby Estate on Sloane Street in Knightsbridge to convince them that they needed us to bring some quality and finesse into the presently tacky Carnaby Estate. We assured them that with our trade contacts we could bring in famous names such as Royal Doulton, Wedgwood, Portmeirion, Belleek and Irish Dresden. Fortunately for us, the landlords were headed up by Peter Bourne, who was working on a plan to improve the area by bringing back artists, designers and one-off quality boutique shops. We fitted the bill and he decided to give us a chance (though he latter admitted that he never expected us to succeed). We were due to open the following week.

Our opening was low key. We could not open our doors with a fanfare as the premises did not have any. There was no shop front, just ugly metal shutters which, on a sunny morning in early August 1986, Robert raised with a flourish.
Looking at each other and grinning we said, "Here we go."
At last we were in business.
I had given in my notice to the Reject China Shop in July and the plan was for me to run The China Ware House on my own for the first month to get some cash flow. Robert would dash across from Beauchamp Place in his lunch hour to give me a break and for the first few weeks, my family: my mum and dad, my Uncle Ted and Aunts Lily and Maisie and Betty and Eunice were mobilized to pop into the shop at various times to give me much needed restroom breaks. It was an "all hands on deck" family start-up operation.
Much to our surprise, Carnaby Street accepted us without much ado and we seamlessly blended into the flow of life on the street. With our focus on quality English made giftware and dinnerware, we were not in direct competition with the other souvenir shops. Within a few weeks, we were delivering on our promise to the landlords by stocking Royal Doulton, Wedgwood, Portmeirion and a multitude of other quality English made brands and introducing a touch of class to the tacky neighborhood.
Visiting tourists from Europe and America wandered in and discovered us, as well as aircrew from TWA. We were on our way and, by September, Robert felt confident enough to hand in his notice so that now we were both working full time in our very own new shop.

Each day was a journey of discovery as we put everything into building up our dream business. Every few weeks, Walter, a friend, would drive me up to Stoke-on-Trent in the Potteries where I would buy a medley of bone china delights, bells, vases, miniature tea sets, whimsical teapots and flowered jewelry from individual craftsmen and potters working in crowded workshops with attached small kilns.

"Safe journey," said Mick and Beryl as we backed the van piled high with gift china out of their small courtyard at "Sheer Elegance."

"See you again in a few weeks," shouted Mick. "I'll have some new ring trees ready to show you then."

"Goodbye," I yelled as the van started to pick up speed and head back to London.

Halfway home on the motorway, we would stop for a meal and I'd always say, "Let's park the van as close to the restaurant windows as possible so I can watch it."

"Sure," Walter would respond, well aware of the nightmare scenario of having someone steal the van with all our precious goods before we could get them back to Carnaby Street.

September and October 1986 seemed to fly by. We were steadily busy and bringing in more stock and had started offering a shipping service to customers not wanting to carry their purchases home. Meanwhile, the construction problems with our designated premises, the listed building at 12 Ganton Street, seemed no closer to solution.

As the days got shorter and winter approached, it started to get colder and colder in the shop which was located at the corner of Carnaby and Ganton Street. The wind seemed to take a particular delight in howling down Ganton Street and straight into our open-fronted store. Layers of sweaters and jackets did not seem to make any difference and something warmer was needed. I had just the thing.

"What on earth are you wearing?" asked Robert as I appeared one morning well-padded from head to toe in green.

"Isn't it great?" I replied. "It's my old ski gear from my trip to Squaw Valley. This will keep me warm."

"You can't wear that," objected Robert. "You look ridiculous. You will make us the laughing stock of the street. We are supposed to be a serious business."

"Okay. But what are we going to do? Everything is going fine and as planned, but for this freezing weather. Do we really want to be so miserably cold?"

"No, you're right. It is unbearably cold. Let's look in the Yellow Pages and ask around the neighborhood and see if we can find someone to put in a glass shop front that's affordable."

And that's how we found Liam, a carpentry genius from Ireland, who could turn his hand to anything involving shop fronts. It was a fluke that we actually found him because he only worked on recommendation and didn't even paint a contact number on his work van. But his quote was affordable and he worked quickly and efficiently and suddenly we were warm again.

With the holiday season approaching, we got busier and Aileen, an artist student friend, started to work with us part-time in the shop.

Peter Bourne and the landlords seemed pleased with our progress and as 1987 and the New Year dawned they requested a meeting with us. The premises at 12 Ganton Street were still not ready and, as we walked into their Sloane Street offices one evening in early January, we wondered what they wanted.

"We have a proposition for you," Peter Bourne launched straight into the subject as soon as we had exchanged greetings. "As you know, we are looking to return The Carnaby Street Estate to its former glory with interesting quality products and we like what you are doing. We are now looking to develop the other side of Ganton Street and have a change of use building there. We are going to convert the big office block to shops at street level and we would like to offer The China Ware House Company the opportunity to move into the double-fronted premises at 14-16 Ganton Street. We are prepared to keep the rent the same as it was going to be for 12 Ganton Street and will pay for our architects to design the storefront. You will just have to get it built. What do you think?"

Robert and I looked at each other in surprised delight.

"Could you give us some time to discuss this?" said Robert.

"Sure," said Peter and left the room with his assistant.

"Well, what do you think?' asked Robert.

We had known that 21 Carnaby Street was only temporary and over the past few weeks, we had begun to realize that we were actually outgrowing 12 Ganton Street without ever occupying it. With its three floors and narrow winding staircases, what had initially seemed an opportunity to get started, was now looking like it might become a liability with floors unable to hold the weight of the china dinnerware and giftware we were actually bringing into stock.

"It's a wonderful opportunity, but it's going to cost us more than we can afford to shop fit it. We will have to approach the bank for a business development loan," I said.

"Okay, but we've discussed this before. We are going to need financing if we are to grow and this is definitely the way forward. Also, don't forget Liam. He will be able to work with us on building the new premises. I say we go for it," Robert responded.

There would be much further discussion of the details, but looking at each other we knew the decision had been made. We would somehow find the financing to move this forward.

A few minutes later, Peter Bourne reappeared followed by his secretary carrying a tray with coffee and biscuits.

"Well, what do you think?" he repeated.

"We like the idea and want to take it forward, but will obviously need some time to sort out the details."

"Good," he smiled. "We can get the ball rolling. Oh, by the way, we have some clients interested in looking at 21 Carnaby Street. Is it okay if I bring them in to show them the premises next week?"

"Sure," we replied confident now that we had suitable premises for The China Ware House Company.

The following Tuesday around midday, Peter Bourne walked into the shop accompanied by two men and a woman who looked distinctly familiar. As they approached the counter, Robert suddenly leaned forward and stretched out his hand to the woman and said, "Now you are a lady whose hand I have wanted to shake for a long time."

She took his hand and smiled with her geometrically cut hair and clothes. It was Mary Quant, one of the originating fashion icons of the swinging sixties and she was looking at our premises.

Carnaby Street was re-emerging once again as a center for Swinging London and Mary Quant was about to move back into the neighborhood with her new cosmetics launch and take over our shop at 21 Carnaby Street, while the China Ware House Company was moving to larger premises. We were on our way.

Three Tattooed Giants

The incident suddenly flashed back in vivid slow motion. I was watching, mesmerized as they swayed back and forth like two saplings in a strong wind. However, these were no saplings, but two very drunk and unkempt leather clad rockers who had stumbled off Carnaby Street into our new temporary shop premises. Our makeshift Habitat shelves were none too stable and were piled high with breakable china goods. A customer who had been browsing, looked up in alarm as the smell of stale beer filled the air and hurriedly left the premises. This was understandable as these huge lumbering drunks seemed to completely take over all the available floor space.

I held my breath as they lurched towards the fragile Belleek Parian china shelf, missing it by a whisker and then back towards the elegant Royal Doulton ladies, who would, if they could, have averted their eyes from such brutish louts. Back and forth they swayed like a slow moving pendulum of a grandfather clock.

"Was I about to witness the demolition of our new chinaware business before we had even gotten started?"

As I stood there transfixed, incapable of movement or speech, Robert, my partner suddenly appeared from the basement as if by magic. Tall, with brown hair and hazel eyes, he had the well-proportioned physique of the male model he had once been. More recently he had handled public relations for some West End nightclubs where emerging stars such as Elton John, then known as Reg Dwight, had started. He was an irresistible charmer and he had a very volatile temper. His cleft chin had a determined look to it as he approached the drunks and I wondered in panic what he was going to do in the very confined space of our shop.

Summing up the scene quickly, he moved slowly and unthreateningly towards the larger of the two drunks. Leaning in towards him, he said something quietly in his ear.

To my amazement, the man tugged on the arm of his drunken friend and started moving towards the street. In a slurred voice, he said, "Sorry mate. No offence intended," as they swayed safely out of the shop and stumbled into the crowds on Carnaby Street.

I stared at Robert in admiration.

"What did you say to them?"

"I suggested that they might feel better out in the fresh air of the street to avoid encountering some pain, something like a broken arm if they inadvertently fell down," he grinned. "I told you my nightclub experience would come in handy."

For some strange reason that incident, which had occurred a few months previously at our old premises at 21 Carnaby Street, had sprung to mind when I heard Robert say, "Vivien come into the shop. There's a situation that I think you should deal with."

I left the office where I had been working on stock orders and followed him onto the shop floor. The store appeared darker than usual. Morning sunlight was streaming through one of the large display windows, but the other window seemed blocked by the black leather backs of what appeared to be three giants.

"What's going on?" I asked.

Moshe, our friendly and efficient sales consultant, came over.

"The three punk rockers out there turned up about half an hour ago and plonked themselves on the window ledge. I waited a while thinking they would move on, but when they didn't, I decided to go and ask them politely to move."

Moshe had grown up in South Africa. His family was originally from India. He had moved to England as a teenager with his mother. He was thirty-six years old, extremely well organized and always impeccably dressed with crisp blue-striped shirts, a bow tie and red suspenders. He was an intuitive salesman with a helpful and friendly way with all people. Nobody could possibly take offence at his manner.

"What did they say?" I asked.

"That they would stay there as long as they wanted, and that I should F off."

"Okay. Robert, it's your turn. You're a tall strong guy, not afraid of anything, go and tell them to get lost."

"That's just the problem," my partner answered. "Unlike last time, these three aren't drunk. If I go out there it's going to ratchet everything up a notch or two and become confrontational. It'll look like I'm challenging them and will probably end in a fight and possibly a broken window and you calling the police. What it needs is somebody small and unthreatening to diplomatically defuse the situation."

I looked at him with dismay. He was right of course and I was going to have to do it.

"Just a minute," I said disappearing into the office to change my sneakers into heels, tuck my T-shirt into my jeans and put on some lipstick to make myself look a bit more fragile and feminine.

"Here goes," I said walking out of the shop to the sound of their wolf whistles.

I sauntered up to the three punks who looked even more menacing from the front than the back. Every surface of visible skin, including muscular arms, was covered by tattoos. They had heavy metal chains around their waists and Doc Martin boots on their feet. Their faces were adorned with spikes and studs through their noses and ears.

"Hey guys," I said in a low friendly voice. "How you doing?"

They stared back at me blankly like I was some irritating buzzing bug.

"You're blocking my window display. Would you please move?"

They glanced at me, looked at each other and laughed, but didn't move.

"Oh come on guys," I said pulling myself up to my full non-threatening height of five feet two. "You're not going to give me a hard time, are you?"

To my complete surprise, the one nearest me suddenly pushed himself off the window ledge saying, "Come on. There's nothing happening here. Let's go to the pub for a beer."

The other two stood up, their chains clinking around their waists. They were huge, nearly seven feet tall and they towered over me, blocking my view of the sky. Talk about Jack and the Beanstalk; I wasn't Jack I was a bean by comparison. To my great relief, they swaggered off, their chains clanking as they ambled down to the pub on the corner of the street.

I walked back into the shop wondering what I would have done if their behavior had matched their looks.

The afternoon meandered by in a flurry of customers and conversations. Around four o'clock, the sound of a Texan drawl caught my attention. A couple was standing in front of the counter which was piled high with an Old Country Rose tea set, Royal Doulton figurines and a selection of fine bone china bells and mugs. The man had a white Stetson and sported a substantial stomach under his red-checkered shirt. His voice carried across the shop as he announced, "This little lady sure is a good saleslady. We just came in to your shop for a few souvenirs and look what she has us buying."

The "Little Lady" was Constance, our part time afternoon sales consultant. Aristocratic in manner, she was aged eighty-nine and was certainly the most persuasive and skilled salesperson we had ever encountered. We had worked together at the Reject China Shop in Beauchamp Place.

When Robert and I moved to these new premises in Ganton Street, we had tempted her out of retirement, saying that we would be delighted if she could just come and sit in the shop and look regal like the queen and chat with customers and answer their questions. Constance loved being with people and had jumped at the opportunity and opted to come in most afternoons for a few hours. She had an amazing ability to elicit information from everybody without giving away any more than a few superficial facts about herself. She had traveled extensively in Germany just before the outbreak of the Second World War and we were convinced that she had been a spy, but however skillfully we tried to broach the subject, she just looked knowingly and quickly changed the topic of conversation.

In the short time she had been working with the couple from Texas, she had established that he was a sheriff from a small town near Austin with two grandchildren (she knew their names and ages), that this was his first visit to England with his wife Betsy to celebrate their fortieth wedding anniversary and that he enjoyed hunting and stock car racing.

"Well I guess that I am going to have to ship this all home," the sheriff said. "We're traveling on to France and Italy in a few days."

"No problem," Constance replied smiling with her blond hair and comfortable brown shoes. "Vivien will help you arrange your shipping order. I hope you both have a wonderful visit here and enjoy your travels. It's lovely to have met you."

With that, she smiled graciously and majestically moved off to help another customer.

"What a lovely lady," Betsy said. "So helpful."

"Yes, she's a real treasure. By the way, how did you find our store? Were you just walking along Carnaby Street?"

"No," replied Betsy. "We found you in our guidebook. Look here you are."

I wasn't aware that we were featured in any guidebooks so I looked with interest as she delved into her handbag and pulled out a book and handed it to me. It was the third edition of Sandra A Gustafsons "Cheap Sleeps in London." I opened the book and looked at it quickly in delight. There it was for all to see.

"Bargain china shoppers used to think the deals were at The Reject China Shop. Now the place to have more fun shopping for chinaware and to get a bargain to boot is The China Ware House Company."

We had done it. The China Ware House Company was now the fun place to shop in London.

Around the World in 101 Days

It all started with a chance comment. I had been dithering for months, indecisive about moving into the co-operative housing project in South London where my sister and two young nephews lived. I had even worked the qualifying thirty-six hours, cleaning and painting one of the apartments, to become a member of the co-operative association. The concept was great, a community of neighbors and friends actively participating to improve their living environment. It was the location that was the problem. Like many Londoners living north of the River Thames, the thought of crossing the river to live in South London was like traveling to a strange and foreign land.

"I've got the answer to your dilemma," said my sister Avril, calling one evening.

"Martin, who lives on the third floor, is off on his travels in March and is looking for somebody to pay the rent for six months. You can move in and try it out and see if you like living here. What do you think?"

"Um," I replied. "That might work."

"Okay." She said. "I'll set up a meeting for the two of you to talk."

We met the following week over dinner at her apartment and spent most of the evening comparing traveling stories. Mine from India and Israel. His from Europe and Australia. Martin was an architect and designer and he had a friendly manner with a good sense of humor. He had decided to take a six month break, leisurely traveling round the world looking at interesting buildings en route to visiting an architect friend in Japan. From there, he planned to journey on to Australia to help another friend start building a house.

The evening flew by in a mixture of talk and wine and soon it was time to leave.

"Well I see you two were getting on like a house on fire. What do you think about moving into his apartment?" asked my sister as I zipped up my leather jacket ready to go.

"Apartment," I looked at her blankly. "I don't know about the apartment, but I wouldn't mind traveling round the world with him. Bye. I'm off home."

I had forgotten all about this casual throw away remark when the phone rang a few days later.

"Hi it's Martin," said the voice at the end of the phone. "I hear you like the idea of seeing the world. Would you like to meet and talk about it?"

How could I resist? The next evening found us chatting over cool glasses of cider in the oak paneled bar at the Red Lion pub on Kingly Street in London's West End and that was the start of several amazing months of planning, deciding which countries to visit and looking at routes and locations. There was never a moment's doubt that this was the trip for me.

My parents were initially scandalized.

"How can you go round the world with someone you hardly know?" asked my father.

"You are going to have to tell the family that you are traveling with a female friend from university," insisted my mother.

"Not a problem," I replied.

However the tactics of getting time off from my work as a department manager at the Reject China Shop in Beauchamp

Place, Knightsbridge, without actually losing my job, required more careful planning. In the end, I decided to just go and speak directly to my boss.

"I need to take some time off."

"How much time?"

"Six months," I replied trying for the maximum.

"Why? Are you ill?" he asked

"No."

"So why do you need the time?"

I looked at him straight in the eye and said, "I want to go around the world."

He stared at me thoughtfully for a long time and finally said, "Okay. You can have three months off without pay and keep your job, but only on one condition."

"What's that?" I asked.

"That you do not let anyone here at The Reject China Shop know what you are doing or else everyone will want to do the same thing."

That seemed reasonable so I immediately thanked him and agreed to his terms and rushed to call Martin.

Thus early March 1982 found us in beautiful San Francisco at the start of our travels. We had hired a car and the plan was to drive to Yosemite and the Grand Canyon and San Diego and then arrive in Los Angeles to catch a flight to Hawaii and onwards to Japan, South Korea, Hong Kong, Macau, China, and Thailand and down the Malay Peninsular to Singapore and Bali. I would then fly back to England via Abu Dhabi, while Martin would continue on to Australia.

We had agreed that Martin would be the driver and I would navigate and I had the day's route sketched on a piece of paper on the dashboard.

"Ready?" asked Martin.

"Let's go," I replied, winding down my window to enjoy the breeze. Martin started to ease the car out of the hotel forecourt, picking up speed as he turned the corner and the piece of paper with the directions flew straight out of the window. I made a grab for it, and missed and watched it soar and disappear. For a moment Martin looked annoyed and then he grinned and asked, "Do we really need it?"

"Of course we don't," I said, "Who needs a road map? We are off to see the world and are free to go where we like when we like for the next three months. When will we ever have such freedom again?

A Passover Seder in Japan

The taxi slowed to a stop. It was evening rush hour in Tokyo. I knew we were in the right neighborhood, as I had seen the name Hiroo on one of the few English road signs, but otherwise I didn't have a clue where we were. What's more is that I had no way of finding out, as my Japanese taxi driver spoke no English.

A Japanese friend had translated the name of the Jewish Community Center into Japanese for me and ever so often the driver turned on the taxi light, asked for the piece of paper I was clutching in my hand, scratched his head, looked at the Tokyo version of A-Z and continued driving. I had heard stories about places being difficult to locate in Japan as there were no specific addresses, only neighborhoods divided into chomes and now it appeared as if this might really be so. How ironic if I was to spend this first night of Passover lost in a Tokyo taxi.

The idea for this evening had occurred a few months earlier when, in the final stages of planning a three and a half month journey around the world, I had realized that I would be in Japan in the Tokyo area for the first night of Pesach.

"Was there a Jewish community there?" I wondered. "If so, how was I to locate it?"

There was no easily accessible Google to hand in the 1980's; however, a note to the travel editor of the "Jewish Chronicle" quickly produced results with details of the community, its minister and location.

Noted and stored for future reference, I had set off on my travels.

Now five weeks into the journey, half way across the world in the land of Shinto and Buddhism, it was suddenly important for me to participate in a Seder. My first telephone call to the Jewish Community Center was from the Ibaraki Prefecture, a region sixty miles outside Tokyo where we were staying with Martin's Japanese friends and was really disappointing.

"Call back tomorrow," I was told. It appeared all the places were taken.

The next day the numbers were still being sorted, but by evening I was told that they were going to squeeze me into the first night's Seder. It was to begin in Beth David, the community synagogue, the next day April 7, 1982, at 6:30 p.m. with a short service followed by the Seder meal in the Community Center.

Suddenly, the taxi jerked and turned off the main road onto a side street. The driver drove on for a few minutes, then stopped and got out of the taxi and crossed the road and stood in front of a board studying a neighborhood map. Once back in the taxi, he drove a little further, stopped and pointed vaguely across the road, indicating that I should get out.

"No way." I couldn't see anything that remotely resembled a synagogue or community center. I wasn't budging or going anywhere. I could see a look of panic begin to appear in his eyes. Was he never going to get rid of this troublesome tourist?

After a moment, he stuck his head out of the window and called out something to a girl who was walking by. She replied with an American accent. By coincidence, she was heading to the same place. I had arrived.

Just around the next corner, the Jewish Community Center was a modern compact building. On the second floor, a crowd was waiting outside the Beth David Synagogue for the service to start. My rescuer turned out to be the daughter of an American family, long based in Japan for business. There seemed to be a lot of Americans around, but I was soon to learn that an American aircraft carrier was in port and its Jewish crew had been invited to participate in the Seder. Both the service and the Seder were to be jointly conducted by the community Rabbi and the Jewish chaplain from the American navy. The short evening service was soon concluded and we adjourned to the large table-filled community hall for the Seder.

It was an interesting mix of people, members of the hundred families that made up the Tokyo Jewish community, crew from the aircraft carrier, visiting Israelis and Americans. There were also some Japanese professors, a woman from Taiwan and a Christian minister, all interested in observing the Seder. Apart from myself, there was only one other English person there, a young English teacher living in Tokyo. Quite a global mix in distinctively different surroundings, yet once the Seder started I was indeed to witness the truth of a statement I had heard so many times in so many places.

"Tonight Jewish people all over the world are observing the same traditional Seder."

The oh-so familiar Seder in Hiroo was the oh-so familiar Seder of Kibbutz Kfar Szold (where I lived for a while) and the oh-so familiar Seder of my home at Sharon Gardens in London. In the midst of the very different cultural surroundings of Japan, here was a familiar traditional oasis, the continuity that linked Jewish people around the world through the centuries. It was a good feeling to be a part of it.

Notes:

Pesach. The Jewish term for Passover.

Passover. The eight-day Jewish spring festival that commemorates the liberation of the Israelites from Egyptian slavery.

Seder. A Jewish ritual and meal that means "order" and marks the start of the Passover festival. The "order" of the evening includes telling the story of the exodus from Egypt, drinking four cups of wine, eating matzah, partaking of symbolic foods placed on the Passover Seder plate and reclining in celebration of freedom.

Matzah. Unleavened bread.

A Thousand Fluttering Blossoms

The water in the deep tub looked warm and inviting. A gentle steam was rising from its clear aquamarine surface. I had prepared myself as instructed, first sitting on a small stool and soaping myself all over and then showering myself thoroughly clean. Now I was ready to experience the wonderful ritual of soaking and relaxing in a hot Japanese bathtub. As I ran my fingers through the shimmering surface, the reflection of my face flickered and whirled and the day's events came flashing back.

We were in Japan staying with Martin's friends: Haruo the architect, his wife Terru, a teacher and their four-year-old son Tommu. We were in the town of Mito in the Iberaki Prefecture, about sixty miles from Tokyo.

Our day had started early. It was the end of term at Tommu's kindergarten and we had been invited to join the celebration for parents, children and teachers. The hall of the school was similar to school halls the world over. A large space with a stage and piano at one end. A table with refreshments stood on one side and seats lined the walls. The hall was decorated with origami carp the children had made.

The program started with thirty excited four-year-olds singing, playing the harmonica, dancing and performing exercises. The clapping of proud parents was followed by a short speech from the head teacher (translated in a whisper for us by Terru) who then invited the parents to come onto the stage and entertain their children. A group of parents, including Haruo and Terru, moved onto the stage to sing and exercise with a ball.

The children, who were seated cross-legged on the wooden floor, clapped politely.

Suddenly, the head teacher was on the stage again and began speaking in halting English, "We are pleased to welcome to our school today visitors from England. We hope you have enjoyed our children's show and we would like to invite you to our stage to perform for them."

Martin turned towards me with a horrified look on his face. I stared back at him in panic. We had had no idea this was going to happen and we had nothing prepared.

"Why didn't you warn us this was going to happen?" Martin hissed at Haruo who was standing there grinning.

"Would you have come if you had known?" he replied. "Go on they'll not bite you."

"What on earth are we going to do?" I asked as the hall, full of parents and children, waited in silence.

"Well, I can't sing. I have a terrible voice. This is awful," Martin said as we wended our way slowly towards the stage.

"Same here. I'm always off key," I responded.

We had reached the stage and there was an expectant silence as we climbed the steps and stood in front of the audience.

"Konnichiwa," said Martin delaying the inevitable.

"Yes, Konnichiwa," I repeated parrot-like.

My desperate memory search for a manageable song had produced just one tune that kept repeating itself. That was going to have to be it.

"Okay. Martin," I whispered. "How about 'London Bridge is Falling Down?' Surely, we can manage that?"

Martin nodded, clenched his fists and closed his eyes.

"Thank you for your kind hospitality," I said my voice shaking slightly. "We have really enjoyed our visit to your school and would like to sing a famous English nursery rhyme for you called, 'London Bridge is Falling Down.' Okay. Martin, here we go. One two, three."

"London Bridge is falling down,
Falling down, falling down.
London Bridge is falling down,
My fair lady."

A discordant cacophony of sound emerged as we painfully forced ourselves to remember the long forgotten verses. It sounded horrible and was really embarrassing, with Martin's low discordant voice merging with my shrill off-note rendition. It seemed to go on forever.

Finally it was over. There was a long silence from the audience followed by polite clapping as we muttered "Arigato, Arigato," and fled from the stage.

Harou was beside himself with laughter. "Wow, that was truly awful. Where did you both learn to make a noise like that?"

"Stop it Harou," Terru said. "Stop winding them up. Look."

The children were all back on the stage. Tommu came to the front and said "Good Morning," in English in a small sweet voice. A teacher began to play the piano and the children started to sing in English, "Head, Shoulders, Knees and Toes" to the same melody of "London Bridge is Falling Down," however, their version sounded musical and delightful. They then ended their performance by singing "Sayonara Martin and Vivien."

It was all so lovely and we realized that we were really thrilled that we had suddenly and unexpectedly become active participants instead of passive spectators.

As I relaxed in the soothing waters of the bathtub, the gentle ripple of the water tickled my shoulders and evoked the memory of our afternoon picnic with the family in a Mito park. Salmon steaks, crisp seaweed, pickled plums and rice cookies under the shade of brilliantly colored cherry trees.

I leaned back and a thousand images of beautiful cherry blossoms and pink fluttering petals seemed to shower down and enfold me. A relaxing end to an enjoyable and different day.

Monsoons and Showers

"All aboard, all aboard!" yelled the guard.
Everybody grabbed their backpacks and rushed to board the Bangkok to Singapore Express. We had disembarked at Pedang Besar, the railway station on the Thai-Malaysia border to go through customs. Backpacks had been emptied and their contents carefully searched by the customs officers who were obviously looking for drugs. We clambered back aboard, our backpacks held close.

As we made our way back to our carriage, we passed the conductor's caboose, a small, compact space with a bed, table, some lockers and a lamp. Each carriage seated about forty travelers with pairs of facing well-worn black leather seats on each side of the aisle.

"Give me your backpack, I'll be able to keep an eye on them here," Martin said, placing the backpacks on the string overhead rack facing him.

"Thanks," I replied, well aware of the danger of unattended bags having drugs slipped into them to be smuggled across the border.

The train was full with a motley crowd of "Lonely Planet" travelers from around the world, a virtual mini "United Nations." We were heading down the Malay Peninsular to Singapore via stops in Penang and Kuala Lumpur.

The train hooted, jerked and began to pick up speed as it left the station.

"Look. It's started to rain," I said, as cooling drops splashed against the half open windows.

"Well, it's the monsoon season," Martin replied.

"Would anyone like some fruit?" asked an American girl sitting a few seats away.

"Not if it's that smelly durian," someone yelled.

"No. I've got mangoes and pineapple," she answered and suddenly everyone in the carriage was reaching into their bags to pull out fruit and snacks to share.

"So, what did you Brits like best about Bangkok?" asked Bill, an Australian leaning across the aisle sucking on a mango stone.

"The Temple of the Emerald Buddha and The Royal Palace," I replied. "I was dazzled by those amazing shapes, colors and golden spires."

"Zipping along the klongs in those narrow wooden boats with souped-up diesel truck engines was pretty cool," said Martin. "What about you?"

"Oh the kick boxers with their speed and acrobatics were my favorites," answered Bill.

"I am going to take a shower," announced Jim, another Australian. "There's already a crowd of people outside the shower cubicle. It's really hot and sticky in here, even with the window open."

He stood up, stripped off his T-shirt and reached into his bag. Then he slung a towel over his bare shoulder and walked off down the aisle in flip-flops and shorts, holding a bar of soap.

We had been traveling for about an hour and the carriage was full of the chatter of travelers exchanging stories and food when the conductor suddenly appeared rushing down the aisle.

"Get up! Get up!" he said stopping in front of the Canadian girl sitting on the opposite side of the aisle in the next row of seats. She looked at him blankly not understanding.

Eyeballing Big Croc

"What did you say?"

"Quick. Stand Up! Stand Up!" he repeated loudly.

Looking puzzled, she stood up. He pushed her to one side and bent down to slide open the bottom of her seat.

The carriage was suddenly silent. All eyes were focused on what was happening.

What was he doing?

The conductor reached down into the space now revealed under the seat and pulled out a large striped shopping bag sealed with a thick transparent plastic cover. Holding it in one hand, he slid back the top of the seat and muttered a brief, "Thank you. Excuse me," and rushed off down the aisle and into the next carriage.

The silence continued for a few seconds and then everyone began to talk at once.

"Did you see that?" said a man with a loud voice and a Swiss accent.

A chorus of replies filled the carriage.

We were all aware that the conductor had his own private cabin on the train where he could store his personal belongings. The bag was something he obviously did not want there; it almost certainly contained drugs. By hiding it under a seat in the open carriage, he had clearly endangered the Canadian girl sitting there. If the customs officers, who had earlier walked through the train, had found the bag, she would have been arrested for this was a time when the Thai and Malay authorities were tightening their drug controls. The very next year in 1983, Malaysia was to introduce the death penalty for drug trafficking as a reaction to the growing drug trade in the region and then proceeded, in subsequent years, to execute both its own citizens and foreign travelers.

Our outrage and alarm at the incident were obvious, and everyone in the carriage now slid open the tops of their seats to check that nothing was hidden in them.

Suddenly, the train slowed for a few minutes as it approached some houses and a junction and then picked up speed again.

"I bet he has thrown that bag off the train," said Bill.

"What can we do?" asked the Canadian girl looking very upset.

"Nothing really," answered Bill. "We don't know who else is involved. It's a good reminder for us always to be vigilant."

The mood in the carriage had definitely changed. It was somber and quiet. The monsoon rain was falling more heavily as the train traveled on its single track past jungle vegetation, small villages and rubber plantations. In some places, it was almost possible to reach out of the train and pick the passing bananas and coconuts.

Suddenly, there was a yell, followed by a string of very colorful English swear words.

What was going on now?

Heads turned to look down the aisle and there, framed in the doorway, was a strange looking Jim. He had bare feet, a skimpy towel tied around his waist and he was covered from head to toe in soap lather.

"The effing water tank has run out of water in the shower. What am I going to do to get this stuff off?"

There was a burst of laughter and the gloomy mood that had been pervading the carriage disappeared as if by magic.

"Well, there's plenty of water outside," joked somebody. "Look at all that rain."

It was true; the rain was now slanting down in large droplets.

"Very funny," retorted Jim. "How does that help me? What am I going to do? I can't get dressed with all this soapy foam."

"Hold on a minute, Jim," grinned Bill, "perhaps we can use nature to help us."

"How?"

"Well, when we come to the next short junction stop, two of us should be able to hold open the train door for you, so you can stand on the wooden ledge that juts out above the steps. You can grab hold of the safety step hold bar and let the monsoon rain wash off the soap. But you had better put on your shorts or you'll be arrested for flapping in the wind."

And that, in reality, was how Jim completed his shower. Helped by friends and precariously balanced on a ledge as the train slowed in its approach to a junction, his soapsuds soon disappeared in the pouring rain, accompanied by peals of laughter and encouraging remarks.

Thus, Jim provided us with a memorable illustration of the fact that when traveling around the world, four vital components are necessary for success: good friends, caution, a sense of humor and a large dose of ingenuity.

Notes:

Durian.
A South Asian fruit with a spiky husk and soft edible yellow fruit. It is regarded by some as a delicacy and by others as stinking and revolting because of its overpowering odor.
Klongs.
 Canals in Bangkok whose banks are lined with houses on stilts, playing children, plants and temples.

Tarantulas, Coconuts and Tropical Sunsets

"I wouldn't go out there if I were you," said Martin one afternoon.

"Why ever not?"

Hot and sticky in a brief bikini, I was covered in sand and I had a towel slung over my shoulder. I was about to go out onto the partially covered terrace where the shower in our thatched cottage was located. It was early June, 1982, and we were on the island of Bali in Indonesia.

"I wouldn't go out there if I were you," he repeated. "Because there's a tarantula out there."

I opened the door cautiously and peered out onto the thatched veranda overlooking the beach. There was nothing remotely creepy-crawly there.

"Stop winding me up, I grinned. " There's nothing there."

"Oh no! Just you wait and see," he said, stretching out on the bed.

The cool water splashed over me as I enjoyed the relaxing panorama of the golden sands and turquoise sea in front of me. *This is the life*, I thought.

As the water washed away the sand and heat, I found myself suddenly feeling uncomfortable, as if something was watching me. Peering through the shower drops, I suddenly became aware of a pair of beady eyes focused in my direction. Turning down the volume of water, I looked at the bricks of the terrace wall and there, blending with the grey texture, was a huge, hairy black-striped tarantula.

Grabbing my towel, I rushed soaking into the room, gasping, "You were right! There really is a tarantula out there."

Martin was lounging on the bed with a smile, obviously waiting for my appearance.

"Told you so," he said with a smirk.

"Okay. I should have listened to you. You were right. Now come and help me get rid of it, so I can finish shampooing my hair."

"Get rid of it! Not me! You know how I hate spiders, and that hairy monster is about twenty times the size of an English spider. Good luck with it."

I stood there dripping puddles on the floor and realizing that Martin really had no intention of moving off the bed. I was going to have to get rid of it myself.

I willed myself to go back out onto the veranda, grabbing a broom on the way out and holding it in front of me like a protective shield. I had to look carefully at the wall to find the tarantula as it had moved slightly higher up the wall and was watching me intently, as if it was calculating what I was going to do. I lifted the broom and with an upward sweep tried to push the hairy beast over the top of the wall and onto the adjoining beach. I failed miserably. The broom thumped harmlessly against the wall, the tarantula was too quick for me and with its eight legs in motion jumped out of the way. It took up a new position, merging into the grey texture of the wall, and its beady eyes continued staring at me as we looked at each other assessing each other's threat. Trying for speed, I suddenly grabbed the shower hose and turned on the water a little too quickly because it spun around out of my hand and ended up soaking me instead of the tarantula. I could almost see it grinning at me, looking so ridiculous standing there in just a towel.

I paused and stared back intently. It was time for a truce. I was, after all, trespassing on its home territory; I was the intruder here, not the tarantula. *What was it going to do? Eat me? I don't think so.* It was time to finish my shower.

I dropped my soggy towel onto the floor and turned on the shower again enjoying the cooling droplets, whereupon, the tarantula, as if acknowledging my retreat, gave a triumphant hop and a jump and disappeared over the top of the wall.

Finishing my shower, I walked back in the room with a self-assured swagger.

"Well, what happened to the tarantula?" queried Martin.

It was my turn to smirk, "Don't worry. I took care of it," I replied.

Bali was idyllic, a real tropical paradise, and the perfect place to end our hundred and one days journey around the world.

We were staying at Kuta Beach with its amazing sunsets, flowered temple processions and friendly people. Sitting on the glorious golden beaches was sheer entertainment as every few minutes, someone would turn up selling puppets, carvings, sarongs, shells, chessboards and relaxing massages. At sunset we relaxed on the curving beach shaped like an amphitheatre soaking up the blazing colors of a tropical sunset.

Our favorite place to eat was Poppies, a lovely garden restaurant with a pool and bridge, fragrant flowers, trelliswork and cane furniture. Dinner was a flavorful treat with avocados, huge tuna steaks in honey, lemon and raison sauce, rice, salad and sherbet, all for an unbelievable five dollars.

After a few days of just lazing on the beach, we decided to explore the island by bemo, an open air minibus with benches instead of seats, and a constant stream of changing passengers: women taking crops to market in baskets and men carrying fighting cocks with brightly colored feathers.

Our first stop was Ubud, an art and craft town in the center of the island. We wandered past terraced rice paddies, a small monkey forest and down a narrow jungle trail to a stream where villagers were bathing under a waterfall. Then onto Kintamani, the town overlooking the volcanic peaks of Mt Batur, and its lake.

Everywhere we went, there were processions of women carrying beautiful flower and fruit arrangements balanced on their heads, offerings for the temples.

At Kalibukbuk next to Lovina Beach on the north side of the island, we stayed in a traditional style Balinese house close to a long black volcanic beach. Meals were served on our veranda, which overlooked a lush tropical garden full of palm trees and ever so often there was the sound of a falling coconut.

The nearby village was home to farmers and fishermen. Late one afternoon as we strolled past the thatched bamboo cottages, we came across a refreshment stall and some tables and chairs tucked away in the shade of coconut laden palm trees.

"Perfect. I can do with a rest in the shade," I said.

"Yes, good idea. I'm thirsty. Let's ask the stall owner to lop off the tops of a couple of green coconuts for us," replied Martin.

The villager approached us with a big smile "Selamat siang, good afternoon. What would you like?"

"Can you open two coconuts for us please, so we can drink the coconut milk?"

The man looked really disappointed and said, "Sorry, we are out of coconuts, but we do have Coca Cola," pointing to a small icebox in the shade of some bushes.

He looked surprised as sitting there under a dozen coconut laden palm trees, we looked at each other in amazement and roared with laughter.

Still, we figured perhaps a couple of coconuts would obligingly drop nearby, preferably not on our heads, while we drank our Coca Colas.

With the end of our travels approaching, we returned to Kuta Beach for a few more days to enjoy the sun and beach.

Then, on June 14, 1982, it was time for us to go our different ways. Martin was traveling on to Australia to visit friends, and, if I wanted to keep my job, I had to catch my flight back to England via Jakarta and Abu Dhabi. My hundred and one days of traveling around the world in perfect freedom were about to end.

A Morning in Kiev with the KGB

"Empty out your handbag."

His voice was low and menacing. His English heavily accented. This was the moment I had been dreading. I was terrified. The next few minutes could affect other people's lives and they were people, in many cases, I didn't even know.

I did have something to hide.

Everything was in slow motion as I took hold of my bag. I was about to play the biggest game of bluff in my life with dire consequences if I blinked at the wrong time.

I dared not look at Jon who was seated just behind me.

Remain Expressionless, remain expressionless, I kept silently repeating to myself. In reality, I was in turmoil, my heart was pumping violently and beads of sweat were forming on my upper lip.

"Empty out your handbag," he repeated in a soft, but insistent tone.

I had known this was going to happen from the moment our morning had been turned on its head. It was 1983 and Jon and I were in the Soviet Union trying to visit refuseniks. These were Russian Jews who wanted to emigrate to Israel and who were harassed by the Soviet authorities once their intentions became known.

That morning, we had been going to visit one such family who lived a bus ride away from our hotel. As we walked towards the entrance of the apartment block, three dark-suited anonymous looking men wearing hats had blocked our way. One of them had asked in heavily accented English, "What are you doing here?"

"Visiting friends of friends," we replied.

"You cannot go into the building," the man said. "You must come back with us to your hotel."

"Why?" Jon asked.

His question was ignored and, although we were not manhandled, the three men moved forward together forcing us back out of the entrance.

"Get in the car," the man ordered.

A big black car with a driver was parked in front of the building.

"Who are you?" I asked not really expecting an answer.

The English speaker flashed some sort of identity badge and uttered a name saying something about National Security. It appeared they were from the KGB or some local national security offshoot. It was clear that we really had no option, but to get in the car. What were we going to do, sprint down the road? Where would we run to?

The English speaker climbed in beside the driver and the two other men positioned themselves next to the doors with Jon and I sandwiched in between. The car picked up speed, the streets of Kiev flashed by and, within minutes, it had come to a stop in front of our hotel.

We were quickly marched through the foyer. The English speaker, obviously the leader of the group, stopped to say something in Russian to the desk clerk who pointed to a door which led to the room where we were now being interviewed.

It was a medium sized nondescript room with a plain wooden table with two chairs and a row of chairs against the wall where Jon, my traveling partner, was sitting holding a plastic bag. The two men stood by the door.

"Empty out the contents of your bag on the table," the interviewer repeated.

Though it seemed like hours, in fact, just a few seconds had passed.

My handbag was filled with the usual traveling necessities like passport, camera, makeup, but the object I was preoccupied with was a wafer-thin miniature notebook with the names and addresses of refuseniks we were attempting to visit in Moscow, Leningrad, Odessa and Kiev. We could not do anything about the apartment we had been going to visit in Kiev– it was either being watched or we had been followed there– but the thought that they might find the other names in the notebook and jeopardize their safety was sickening.

Jon lived in Birmingham and I was from London and we had been friends for many years. We had heard about refuseniks on the news and at our respective synagogues where there were lists of people who liked contact from Jewish people once they became refuseniks. So we had noted the names of some families to visit and I had miniaturized the details in a tiny notebook that I had hidden behind one of my credit cards.

Willing my hand not to shake and clenching the muscles of my face to remain expressionless, I reached into my bag and threw some keys on the table followed by my passport. Then my hand seemed to take on a life of its own and I found myself reaching for my credit card wallet and skimming it across the table towards my anonymous interviewer. In this cat and mouse game, what was the point of playing the apprehensive mouse and leaving the notebook to last, making it obvious that I was trying to hide it?

I forced myself to look nonchalant as the bureaucrat reached for the black leather credit card case and opened it.

"Ah," he exclaimed. "The credit cards every rich English tourist uses."

"No," I corrected him amazed that my voice was steady. "These are the credit cards every poor English tourist uses."

He shrugged and to my incredible relief, threw the wallet back on the table without taking the Visa and MasterCard out of the case.

I bent my head over my bag so he could not see the absolute relief that was zinging across my face and rapidly emptied out the rest of the contents of my bag: lipstick, mirror, brush and comb, map, pen and a variety of other odds and ends. Nothing to fear here. I tipped it upside down and shook it with a final flourish.

"Okay. You can put everything back," he said, dismissing me with a wave of his hand.

"Go and sit over there." He pointed to where Jon was sitting and beckoned him to the table.

Jon gave me an encouraging grin and placidly walked to the table.

"What's in that bag?" he demanded pointing to the plastic bag Jon was holding.

"Spare jeans," Jon replied.

"Take them out."

Jon slowly opened the bag, took out the Levi's and put them on the table.

"I see you are going to sell these trousers on the black market," the man stated.

"No, I'm not." Jon responded.

"Well, why are you walking around town with them if not to sell them?" the man insisted.

"In case the zip on my trousers breaks. I always carry a spare pair for emergencies."

"You're just saying that," the interviewer replied sounding somewhat exasperated. "You don't expect me to believe that you walk around England carrying a spare pair of trousers all the time?"

"Yes I do. I always carry a spare pair in my car in Birmingham," Jon replied in his quiet pragmatic way.

That was his story and he was sticking to it and, when Jon makes up his mind, there's no moving him.

After another ten minutes or so, the interviewer seemed to lose interest in us. He muttered something to the two silent men standing by the door in Russian and then said to us, "You can go."

No explanation, no apology just, "You can go."

Still, we were not about to stand around and argue with him.

He ushered us out of the room into the hotel foyer, said something to the clerk at the desk and then all three men disappeared.

Jon gripped my hand and whispered out of the side of his mouth, "Act normal."

"Act normal?" I wanted to jump up and down with relief, but I didn't.

"Let's go up to our room," I suggested.

Once there, we turned on the radio loudly and went into the bathroom where we turned on the shower and all the taps. We had previously been warned that the rooms might be bugged, but had not taken such things seriously. Now–we were not so sure. Then we flopped down on the bed to discuss the day's events.

The next day, our third day in Kiev, we decided that we should not attempt to visit anyone else, but would be tourists and explore Kiev, so after a leisurely breakfast we walked out of the hotel towards the main square. First we passed a farmers market which, in contrast to the other cities we had visited, had a large array of fresh fruit and vegetables. As we wandered among the stalls, I had a sense of movement behind me.

"Jon, I think we are being followed."

"Oh, come on Viv. Don't be paranoid," he said. "It's your vivid imagination."

We walked past some shop windows with 1950's style suits and dresses and I was sure I caught sight of a couple's reflection and it was not ours.

"We're being followed," I insisted.

"Prove it," said Jon.

"Okay." I said rising to the challenge. "You see that next turning?" I said, pointing to an upcoming street. "Turn right when we reach it."

At the corner, we turned right into a street of uniform squat apartments.

"Let's walk and count to fifty and then turn round quickly and retrace our steps," I said.

"All right," said Jon obviously humoring me. "I still think you are imagining this."

We continued walking and, on the count of fifty, turned round sharply and came face to face with a man and a woman walking a couple of yards behind us and cruising behind them was a small grey car.

"Dasvidania...Goodbye," I said as we walked past the couple who momentarily looked uncertain what to do.

"Well," I said triumphantly to Jon. "Was I right?

Jon glanced back after a few moments and saw that the couple and car had also changed direction and were trailing after us.

"Okay. I was wrong," he admitted. "They are following us."

"Let's have some fun then," I suggested and, for the rest of the day, we led them a merry dance taking them on a tour of the sights of Kiev, its streets, churches, parks and museums at times turning and waving to them. We finally lost them late in the afternoon as we walked round Kiev's main square Maidan Nezalezhnosti (Independence Square) for the fifth time and then disappeared into the large department store that stood on one side of it. By this time, we presumed they had realized they were wasting their time.

This was our third and last day in Kiev.

On our first day in the city, we had decided that we had to visit Babi Yar, the ravine that was the site of the massacre of thousands of Jews by the Nazi's in the Second World War. We had heard that there was nothing at the site to mark what had occurred there and thought it important to bear witness to its existence.

Not unexpectedly though, tour buses were available for many excursions, none could be found for this sad journey so we joined with some Christian visitors to hire a taxi to get to the ravine.

The poet Yevtushenko was right for, at the time of our visit in the early 1980's, it was as he had written,

Over Babi Yar
There are no memorials
And everything is one silent cry.

The massacre site was grassed over with not one marker or stone to record the horrors that had occurred there, to remember the thousands of Jews and non-Jews buried at the site. All we could do was to cry the words "Am Yisrael Chai, The People of Israel are alive," as we stood in silent homage to our people.

It was a relief to leave Kiev; it seemed to me to be a place where I could feel the intolerance of centuries, as if pogroms and anti-Semitism were lurking just around the corner. I had felt uncomfortable all the time I was there and never wanted to return.

In contrast, I had not felt the same in the other cities we visited. St. Petersburg (Leningrad as it was called then) had grace and culture, Moscow was a bustling city with the fascinating Kremlin area, Odessa seemed a warmer, more emotional type of city and I had gotten to climb the Potemkin Steps.

All in all, to be in the Soviet Union in this pre-Glasnost and Perestroika era was a strange and unsettling experience.

After two weeks of visiting refuseniks and sightseeing, it was time to fly home. The return journey from Moscow was a mirror of our arrival. On that occasion I had sped through passport control, while Jon had been delayed and all the prayer books and Jewish literature we were bringing had been confiscated.

This time, on the way out, he went through without a problem and it was I who was stopped.

"What's in your case?" the customs officer asked.

"Just clothes and some Babushka dolls for presents," I replied.

"Open it," he ordered.

Then, for the next thirty minutes, he painstakingly went through everything. All the other people on my flight disappeared and I was the only passenger left there.

"My flight's about to leave. You can see there's nothing there. Why can't I go through?" I asked beginning to feel panicky and terrified that the flight would leave without me and I would be left alone in this unfriendly country. Who knows what might happen. I might be accused of being a spy or a drug dealer. My imagination was beginning to work overtime. The customs officer had picked up my camera and some rolls of film.

"What's on this film?" he demanded.

"Just usual tourist photos," I replied.

He disappeared for a moment only to reappear with another customs official who appeared to have a higher ranking.

He asked me the same question.

"What's on this film?"

"Just usual tourist photos, buildings and some friendly people we met during our visit," I said.

"You can't leave the country with this film," he stated. "We are going to confiscate it."

At this stage, I didn't care if they confiscated everything just as long as I could catch my flight.

He took the rolls of film and the roll from the camera and said, "You can go now."

I snapped the case shut, grabbed it and started running in the direction the other passengers had gone towards the gate. Surely it would be closed. It was just five minutes to flight time. A crewmember opened a door and pointed to the steps of the plane and there, wedged in the doorway, I could see Jon, his back pressed against the side.

"Come on slowcoach," he yelled.

I ran up the steps lugging my case which he took from me, pulling me behind him towards a seat. I was shaking and could not stop the trembling.

He put his arm round me and said, "Come on, Viv. It's okay now. We're leaving."

The airplane door banged shut and the engines started to sound and the plane began to move.

I found out later that Jon had wedged himself in the doorway refusing to let the crew close it until I was on board.

As the plane soared upward, I turned to Jon and said,

"Thank goodness we're leaving. Nothing will ever get me back into this part of the world again."

However, *never say never.*

More than twenty years later we were to return to the area under very different circumstances.

But that's another story.

Notes:

Babi Yar.
The disgraceful ignoring of the events of history of the massacre at Babi Yar has now changed and, in recent years, memorials to the victims of these tragic events have been put up.

The Potemkin Steps.
They are considered a formal entrance into Odessa from the direction of the sea. They were made famous in Sergei Eisenstein's 1925 silent film, *The Battleship Potemkin.*

Babushka doll.
A set of dolls of decreasing size placed one inside another. The correct Russian name for these nesting dolls is Matryoshka dolls.

Confiscated film.
Once back in England, I contacted the Foreign Office with details of what had occurred. They tried for nearly a year to get the photos back, but with no success as the Russians eventually said they had destroyed the film.

A Hug Encircling the World

"Do you want the good news first or the bad?" asked my eighty-nine-year-old father on his birthday from his hospital bed. It was April 8, 2003.

"The bad," I replied, wanting to get the negative out of the way as quickly as possible so I could rebuild on the positive.

The bad news was immediately clear and obvious.

My father, always confident and in charge of situations, had confronted his consultant that morning and demanded to know if he was going to be able to proceed with his plan to move to California in the coming months.

The answer had been a brief, but to the point, "No."

Having been in the hospital for a week as an emergency admittance with failing kidneys in urgent need of new stents and a heart too weak to withstand the procedure, this answer was a confirmation for him rather than a surprise.

Regarding the so-called, *good news,* I cannot recall, even to this day, which of the following actually qualified for that description.

Perhaps it was, "They have found me a bed in a ward upstairs and so I can move from this tiny annex in the emergency section."

Or more likely it was my father looking at me directly and saying, "I've come to a decision."

"What's that?" I asked, not certain what to expect, but certainly not the words that were about to follow.

"I want to be buried in America," he replied.

I looked at him aghast, wanting him alive, not wishing to go anywhere near this subject not even to say the word. But I had to.

"You want to be buried in America," I exclaimed. "Why? You've never mentioned this before."

He looked at me wisely.

"Well if all the family is going to be in California, I want to be there too."

This was a reference to the fact that my sister Avril was married to a New Yorker, Bob Brodey, and lived with the grandchildren, Daniel and Thomas, in San Francisco. My mother and father had received their green cards and mine was about to come through. We had been planning to make the move as soon as we could sell our house in London.

"Are you sure?" I asked, thinking of the strong links he had to the local Jewish community at the Hackney and East London Synagogue, affectionately known as *Brenthouse Road Shul* where he had been a warden for the past twenty-one years.

"Yes," he replied.

"But how on earth could something like that be arranged quickly?"

My father, who always liked giving his two daughters a good challenge, looked at me and actually grinned.

"Oh, you'll find a way. You are, after all, my daughter."

He had obviously made up his mind about the subject so there was no point in arguing the matter. But I was the only one who knew. How would my mother and the family react? They might even think I was making it up.

Later that evening recounting the conversation to my mother, she was as surprised as I had been.

"When did he decide this?" she asked.
"Apparently today after speaking to the doctor."
"How on earth could we do that?"
"I haven't got a clue," I replied. "Let's discuss it with him again when we next visit."

And we left the matter there.

That night I woke up at 4:00 a.m. My sister, Avril, was planning to come and visit my father in a few weeks in early May, but I suddenly had a strong feeling in my gut that she should come now. It was 8:00 p.m. in California so I phoned and told her of dad's deteriorating condition.

"I'll try and get a flight and come immediately," she said.

A few hours later, she called to say she would be arriving the next day and would go straight to the hospital.

My father's face lit up with pleasure as she walked in the next day. Later, as we sat round his bed chatting, I decided to broach the subject.

"Dad, you said the other day that you want to be buried in America. Would you like to confirm that to the family?"

"Yes, I do. Definitely," he said.

And that was the end of the conversation with all of us hoping it was something we would not have to think about for some time.

Sadly, that was not to be.

Avril's visit was intended to be just a short four days. She ran a landscape gardening business with my brother-in-law, Bob in San Francisco and was booked to return home on Tuesday.

It was decided that she would spend the day on Monday at the hospital with my mother, while I went to my office in the morning. At the time, I was working for a media company in North London on a Global Corporate Social Responsibility publication. I left the building in Golders Green at around 2:00 p.m., just missing the call and message that would be the first message I would gut-wrenchingly hear, four weeks later, on my return.

"Viv come to the hospital immediately."

Not aware of any particular emergency, I didn't hurry to the hospital, knowing they preferred afternoon visitors to arrive after 3:00 p.m.

I arrived as planned at 3:00 p.m. and, on reaching the ward and seeing the drawn curtains, I immediately knew something was wrong. My father had passed away in the last thirty minutes. My mother and sister were sitting there in shock.

We held each other tightly in tears, looking at my dear dad, the warrior, the organizer, the man who got things done, our beloved father lying there so still and silent.

It was Monday, April 14, three days before the Jewish Festival of Passover, which began with the first Seder at nightfall on Wednesday, April 16. How on earth were we going to halachically fulfill my father's wishes of being buried in California before the onset of Pesach just two days away?

It was just impossible. It couldn't be done.

Avril and I looked at each other.

Yes it could. It had to be possible.

After all, we were our father's daughters.

As soon as we got home, Avril phoned Bob to tell him what had happened so he could start enquiries about an appropriate orthodox Jewish burial ground somewhere in the Bay Area.

Brenthouse Road Shul knew what had happened as Naftali Tiefenbrun, the minister and cantor who was particularly close to my father, had immediately come to the hospital when we called him. Years before, my father had given me a list of things to do in just this situation. But how were we going to get him to the United States in just two days?

Then our friend, Betty, the efficient administrator at the synagogue came up with the name of a facilitator, Samuel Shalom. He ran a travel business in the City of London and, as a mitzvah, also facilitated Jewish burials in Israel and other parts of the world. We contacted him and he agreed to see us first thing the next day.

Early the next morning in his office, he explained that it was indeed possible as long as we could get him the necessary paper work, the death certificate and green body release form quickly that day. He would organize all necessary matters with the U.S. embassy. A flight for my father's body could be arranged for early Wednesday morning. The fact that California was eight hours behind the United Kingdom time-wise meant this could be done before the onset of the Passover holiday.

Our family would have to immediately book a flight so we could travel to the United States the next day. We would also have to give him the details regarding the Chevra Kadisha, who would be receiving my father's body in America.

I explained that my father had requested that his body be driven past the Hackney and East London Synagogue before he was taken to the airport. Samuel said it would be possible later that afternoon on the way to Heathrow Airport as long as we got him the necessary documents in time.

The amount he charged for this amazing service was incredibly reasonable.

We left his office and jumped into a taxi.

"Where to first?" asked Avril.

"Hackney Hospital to collect the medical certificate of cause of death and then on to Hackney Town Hall," I replied.

At the hospital, we asked the taxi driver to wait, quickly collecting the necessary medical certificate from a doctor.

"Hackney Town Hall next," I said as we got back in the taxi.

It was still early, around 9:00 a.m., and the office of the Register of Births, Deaths and Marriages had just opened as we arrived.

We had assumed, as Hackney had a large Jewish population, that there would be an understanding of Jewish burial procedures and the need for speed and that there would be a section that facilitated a quick process. However, no such section existed. We were told there were some people before us, as well as previously arranged appointments, and we would have to wait.

"How long will it take?" my sister asked.

"No idea," was the unhelpful answer of the clerk.

"Can we speak to the manager?"

He came out from his office and said the same thing.

"We have previously arranged appointments."

"But this is an emergency," I explained. "We need to get my father's body to the United States by tomorrow."

"Sorry," he replied, "but you are still going to have to wait."

A woman, who was filing some papers, looked in our direction and gave us a sympathetic smile.

And so we sat there waiting for over an hour growing tenser and tenser as other peoples names were called and we watched them disappear into back offices.

With rising blood pressure and mounting alarm, we realized that Hackney Borough bureaucracy could stop everything from happening the way it needed to.

Suddenly, the woman who had been filing papers earlier appeared and called our names, smiled and showed us to her office and started processing our information quickly and efficiently. She had heard what was happening and had given up her coffee break to help us. We thanked her profusely.

With the required paperwork in hand, we hailed another taxi and rushed back to Samuel's office to give him the death certificate and green form needed to move things forward.

Then we headed home to follow up on the necessary phone calls and to pack for the flight the next day to the United States.

It was amazing the way everything now began to fall into place.

Bob had worked wonders and found "The Home of Peace," an orthodox Jewish cemetery owned by the Beth Jacob Congregation in Oakland. They had agreed to organize the burial.

Our minister and cantor Naftali, on being told of this, phoned Rabbi Judah Dardick, the Rabbi of Beth Jacob, to tell him about my father, his commitment to and involvement with the Shul and Jewish community, to convey an idea of the man behind the name.

Later that day, Rabbi Dardick called the family from California and spent an hour talking to my mother, sister and me, asking about my father so he could personalize his oration and feel closer to this man whom he had never met.

At just after 5:00 p.m. there was a call from Samuel Shalom. Everything was arranged and in order and he would be driving my father's body past Brenthouse Road Shul in about forty-five minutes.

We immediately phoned Naftali and Betty at the Shul to tell them what was happening, but with such short notice, we thought that there was not enough time for the community to get there.

My mother, sister and me immediately got in our cousin Monty Richardson's car and drove to Brenthouse Road.

When we arrived, the doors and gates of the synagogue were open and all the lights in the shul were on just as my father had requested. Standing silently on the steps outside, were Betty and Gerald, Stephen, Alan Greenblat, Leana and Joe, Ivor and Ron. Gradually more and more members of the community appeared quietly, as if by magic. Naftali arrived with his father and eldest son and Rabbi Potash and Rabbi Shaw. We had a minyan. More friends came, standing quietly aware that this was the moment to pay their last respects to their "Beloved Monty" in the United Kingdom. A short and meaningful service was held on the steps and then the car carrying my father began to move slowly past the shul and down Brenthouse Road.

Silently, the family and community of friends linked arms in a giant all-encompassing hug and followed it down to the end of the road where it stopped for a moment, turned the corner and disappeared in the evening traffic.

The next day, the timing of the two flights was amazingly synchronized. Our flight made possible by customer friendly Virgin Atlantic arrived just thirty minutes after the British Airways flight carrying my father's body. It was 1:30 p.m. on Wednesday, April 16.

Bob was there to meet us with Daniel and Thomas. It was like the rounding of the circle, with my father's friends at the Hackney and East London Synagogue waving him off and his family in California now welcoming him.

After a quick coffee, we immediately set out on the drive to Oakland to "The Home of Peace." Everything was happening so quickly, there was no time to feel exhausted after our ten-hour flight. We drove across the Bay Bridge to Oakland and forty minutes later, we arrived at 'The Home of Peace," an oasis of quiet garden in the city.

Gathered there were family and friends from Avril and Bob's Beit Tikkun community. There were far more people than we had expected, but then many of them had met and known my father from his many visits to the Bay Area.

Rabbi Dardick came forward to introduce himself. He had brought members of his Beit Jacob community. It was remarkable that everyone had come so willingly, so close to the start of Pesach.

Then the moving service started and we were able to fulfill my father's wishes halachically just before the onset of Pesach with his beloved grandsons, Daniel and Thomas, and great-grandsons, three-year-old Daniel and one-year-old Jacob able to participate.

As his grandsons helped him to his final resting place, the reason for my father's request was abundantly clear.

The linked and comforting arms of our family and many friends here in California now joined with those of the Brenthouse Road community to circle the world in an all embracing hug.

Notes:

Warden.	A person who assists in the running of the synagogue service.
Shul.	Synagogue.
Halachically.	According to Jewish Law.
Pesach.	Jewish term for the Passover festival.
Mitzvah.	A good deed done from religious duty.
Chevra Kadisha.	Jewish burial society.
Minyan.	A quorum of ten adult Jewish men required for traditional Jewish prayer.

A Torah Returns Home to Baranovichi in Belarus

As the two policemen goose-stepped through the entrance of Minsk Airport, my stomach churned and a wave of fear and paranoia began to sweep over me as long forgotten memories began to surge.

Twenty years earlier, following a tumultuous visit to Jewish refusniks in Russia, I had sworn never to return to this part of the world again. Yet here I now was, standing in Minsk International Airport in Belarus.

It was November 19, 2003.

Earlier that year in April 2003, my beloved father Monty Zielin had passed away. He was an active man imbued with a love of his family, friends and community and the family had wanted to find a relevant way to honor his memory. After much thought we had come up with the idea of donating a Torah to a re-emerging Jewish community in Eastern Europe. This seemed particularly relevant to my mother, Ivy, my sister, Avril and myself as my father had been actively involved in sending a Torah to Poland a few years earlier. He would definitely have approved of this plan.

My sister Avril, always "the doer," started searching for a Torah that we could afford in the vicinity of San Francisco where she lived with her husband, Bob Brodey. She was pointed in the direction of Rabbi Shmuel Miller, a scribe based in Los Angeles. She called him and told him of our search.

He, in turn, told her of a very special Torah that had come into his possession.

Truly a "Tree of Life," it had amazingly survived the horrors of wartime Europe. Originally belonging to a synagogue in Poland, it had been rescued before the outbreak of the Second World War and sent to London for safekeeping where it had been used for some years and then somehow had made its way to America for Rabbi Miller's safekeeping and refurbishment.

On hearing about this Torah, Avril immediately called my mother and myself.

"I've found it!" she said excitedly. " A Torah that needs to go home. Dad would be so thrilled to be a part of this. Shall we go ahead?"

"Yes," my mother immediately replied.

"Absolutely," I concurred.

This was indeed our father's Torah. We could return it to its home territory in a circle of life.

It was agreed that Avril and Bob would fly to Los Angeles to collect the Torah the following week. Bob, meanwhile, ordered a special blue velvet cover for the Torah embroidered in Hebrew with my fathers name and the words, "The Tree of Life."

At the same time, Avril and Bob had contacted the Bay Area Jewish Rescue Group for Soviet Jews for help in finding an appropriate home for the Torah. It was now that Larissa, a key facilitator for the project, came onto the scene. She had a wide knowledge of Jewish communities in Poland, Russia and Belarus. One particular community stood out for her, a re-emerging community in the town of Baranovichi in Belarus.

During the Second World War, its Jewish population of 12,000 had been forced into the Baranovichi ghetto and most had not survived. However, some adults and children had managed to escape into the forests to hide with the partisans. After the war ended, survivors had moved back into the area and now were proudly reasserting their "Jewishness" with a great thirst to learn more.

Larissa had visited the community the previous year with a group from Congregation Beth Emek in Livermore and felt that the Jewish Community, "Shalom" in Baranovichi in The Republic of Belarus, was an appropriate home for the Torah.

In early September, Avril called to update us on her search. As my enquiries in England to find a home for the Torah had produced mainly established communities in Poland, we all now agreed that Baranovichi was the place we were looking for.

"What about visas?" I asked. "Do we need them?"

"Yes. Larissa will organize them for us," she replied.

"How are we going to communicate with people?" Since none of us spoke Belarusian, language was obviously going to be a problem.

"Larissa knows an interpreter who lives in Minsk. She will meet us at the airport and travel with us."

It was all settled. We had the Torah and now the community; all that remained was to book the flights to Belarus so we could all link up.

"We," being Avril and Bob flying in from San Francisco, myself from London and my friend Jon who lived in the English City of Birmingham. He had traveled to Russia with me twenty years earlier and I had invited him to join us.

My mother was very much an important part of this project and she fully participated in all the discussions. However, at the age of eighty-seven, she understandably felt unable to make the long journey.

"Don't forget to tell the Jewish community in Baranovichi what a wonderful man your father was—how he fought in the British army in the Second World War and was an active member of his synagogue, how he was a kind and wise person," she instructed me as I prepared to leave.

Thus, it was on the morning of Thursday, November 19, 2003, that the four of us met in the departure lounge at Heathrow Airport. There, in a protective case on a seat, was the Torah. Amazingly, Avril and Bob had insisted and been allowed to carry it aboard their flight from America at a time when everything was being checked. For the rest of the journey, this continued to be the same as we took turns to hand carry it home.

"BA Flight 0700 to Vienna now boarding," the loudspeaker announced.

"That's us," said Bob. "Let's go."

Following a two-hour flight, we landed in Vienna where we joined a charter flight to Minsk. It was a small plane with very cramped seats and our knees almost touched our chins, but the Torah still came aboard and was not checked in.

A few hours later, four heavily coated visitors disembarked at Minsk airport. Waiting to meet us, was Tanya, our interpreter—our lifeline—without whom nothing could have been achieved because (with very few exceptions) nobody we encountered spoke English or anything other than Belarusian, Russian or a few words of Hebrew or Yiddish.

"It's still in Vienna. Can you believe it? They've left my case behind," Jon's voice brought me back to the present. He had been waiting for his luggage which had not been unloaded with our three bags.

How strange, I thought. *What was it with me and Jon in East European airports?* Twenty years earlier at St Petersburg (then Leningrad) airport, Jon had been delayed by customs, where officers had confiscated all the Passover books and literature we had been bringing in for refusniks. Then, on the way out of Moscow Airport, I had been held back until the last moment by the authorities going through my luggage with a fine-tooth comb and confiscating all my photographs. Now here we were, again delayed, this time by the inconvenience of a lost case.

Hold on, I realized. *What does it matter? The important fact was that nobody had stopped us from bringing in the Torah. This time it was going to be different.*

"Never mind Jon," said Bob. "I can lend you a shirt and sweater and we can go shopping for some basics as soon as we get settled. We are, after all, only here for four days."

The drive into Minsk from the airport took about thirty minutes. Tanya had arranged for us to stay in the apartment next to hers in central Minsk. It belonged to a neighbor who was away in the countryside visiting relatives.

That evening, as we strolled through the snow-lined streets of Minsk clad in thick coats and woolly hats, warm protection against the chill air, we were surprised by the elegance of the city, the wide boulevards, broad river, grand buildings and squares. We appeared to be the only foreign visitors. Belarus did not encourage visitors from the West, governed as it is to this very day by the autocratic dictator Alexander Lukashenko.

We had dinner in a warm and cozy restaurant and enjoyed being serenaded by a group of musicians with accordions playing Belarusian tunes. We then went shopping in a traditional style department store with long glass display counters and walls decorated with patriotic painted panels for Jon's missing necessities and had fun trying on the traditional fur hats. On the walk back to the apartment, one brightly lit window attracted our attention. Unusually, a long line of people were waiting outside. Inside, it was full of smiling children.

"Bet that's a McDonald's," said Bob in jest as we approached it.

As we got closer, we realized he was right and that, ironically, this was the only obvious sign of any foreign influence in the city that we had seen.

Early the next morning, awoken by the clanking of the bold brass pipes which stood guard against the harsh outside cold, we enjoyed a traditional breakfast of Draniki (fried potato pancakes), sour cream and tea and set out on the journey to travel to the town of Baranovichi some seventy-eight miles away.

As we boarded the train that was to take us on our way, we entered a bygone age of travel. It was an iron monster and with its vast engine and grand carriages, it evoked images of Doctor

Zhivago. Each carriage sported black upholstered seats, overhead bunks and pull down blinds. At the end of each carriage stood a samovar which delivered steaming black tea into glasses with decorative nickel-plated holders. The conductor pulled up the carriage steps, a whistle blew and the monster began to move.

Minsk was soon left behind and the scenery raced by, flat and forested without any contours of hills, its lack of defensible borders a clear indication of how easy it had been for surrounding countries to grab territory and overrun the country over the ages.

An hour or so sped by and the train began to slow as we approached our stop. With a loud screech of the brakes, the locomotive came to a halt and there, standing on the long empty platform wrapped in warm coats and scarves, was a small group of people. It was our welcoming committee from the Baranovichi Jewish Community, the friendly faces of Nadia, the Shalom club director and Ludmila, its strong minded and determined leader.

"Welcome to our town," said Ludmila, as Tanya quickly translated. "We are happy to see you."

"Thank you. We are happy to be here," we chorused in reply.

"It's not very far into the center of the town. We thought you might like to walk if your cases are not too heavy. Would that be okay?" continued Ludmila.

"Yes," Avril replied. "It will give us a chance to get our bearings."

With Tanya by our side spontaneously translating, the conversation flowed seamlessly, as it was to do throughout the whole trip. Her eloquent skills made this whole trip possible. With short blond hair, blue eyes and a friendly smile, she worked with Yacov Basin as a secretary interpreter at "The Union of Councils for Soviet Jews, Representation in the Republic of Belarus" and was very quickly to become a close friend.

As we walked across the metal bridge spanning the tracks of this railway junction station and started making our way through the outskirts of the town with Ludmila leading, followed by Avril and Bob carrying the Torah, I began to get the feel of what the Shtetl of my grandparents might have looked like. Small wooden houses with fences dotted the streets with chickens and dogs in some of the gardens. The air was crisp. Gradually the mud streets were replaced by pavement and the landscape began to change as we approached the modern town with its monotonous rows of apartment buildings, three or four stories high, painted in dull gray and beige. They were definitely more utilitarian than elegant.

We had been invited to stay with members of the community and were warmly welcomed into the home of Ludmila's son and daughter-in-law, Sergey and Leana and their young daughter Katyusha for refreshments and a meal. It was a friendly, casual and very enjoyable evening as we sat around the table getting to know each other and exchanging stories. Avril and Bob were going to stay in their apartment, while later that evening Tanya, Jon and myself traveled by taxi to stay with Nadia and her husband Edik and their two sons, Sanya and Dima, in their house on the outskirts of the town.

The next morning found us standing silently in front of the memorial stone for the Baranovichi Ghetto in Tsaryuka Street, reading its inscription:

"Located in the town in 1941-1942 was a Jewish ghetto to which 12,000 citizens fell victim."

A cold silent witness to atrocities too terrible to forget that had occurred there, yet somehow totally incapable of conveying the sheer enormity of the horror and brutality that those 12,000 innocent citizens must have endured crammed into the streets of the ghetto that had stood on this now neat grassy antiseptic spot.

However, on the other side of this small-grassed memorial, was a shining symbol of hope and survival. Standing in front of a small community building, were a group of elderly men and women. Yanina, one of the women was holding a silver tray with a round harvest loaf and a pot of salt to welcome us in traditional style.

The group was "The Association of Former Prisoners of the Ghetto" which included "The Children of the Ghetto."

We were invited into the building to have lunch with them. With Tanya translating, we sat around the table mesmerized as they recounted their stories of survival during those terrible times. Now in their seventies and eighties, they had, as children, either escaped or been smuggled out of the ghetto to live in the forests with the partisans, surviving the hardships and horror bearing witness for future generations. At times when the translation got left behind and neither side could actually understand the words being spoken, there was an indescribable spark of communication and emotional understanding that illuminated the raw energy and unity of shared communal memory.

That Shabbat evening November 21, 2003, "The Community Club of Jewish Culture Shalom" which served as a center for the Jewish community of Baranovichi, was alive with laughter and joy as the community came together to celebrate the arrival of the Torah. The hall was filled with chattering adults, dancing children and tables invisible under a feast of food, gefilte fish, herrings, potato latkes, eggs, salads, challah, olives, pickled cucumbers, sour cream, cheeses and chocolate babka.

Also there, was Yacov Basin who was head of the "Union of Councils for Soviet Jews Representation in the Republic of Belarus," Yanina Demyanets, Chair of "The Association of the Former Prisoners of the Ghetto" and various Baranovichi town officials. Rabbi Grisha Abramovitch, a young rabbi from Minsk, had arrived to conduct the Shabbat service.

Ludmila Maltseva, the active leader of the community, acted as "The Master of Ceremonies," introducing the children who sang so beautifully in Ivrit, teenagers who performed Israeli dances, a group who performed national dances to klezmer music as well as a range of speakers from the community and the town.

Avril and myself gave emotional speeches, beautifully translated by Tanya, talking about our father, Monty, who had been a warden of "The Hackney and East London Synagogue" in London for twenty-one years, and whose memory we wanted to honor by presenting the Torah to the community. We had brought a photograph of him wearing his army medals from his service in the British Army during the Second World War and it was particularly poignant to see some of the older men in the community also wearing their Second World War medals.

As I stood there holding his photograph, I could feel so strongly the connecting link between these Jewish men who had lived thousands of miles apart, yet had shared a common purpose in different armies in defeating the forces of destruction. It was truly moving.

I finished my speech with the words, "Our family is presenting this Torah to your community in memory of our father, Monty Zielin. A few years ago he was involved in sending a Torah to a community in Poland and I know how much he would have loved to be here and to be a part of the renaissance and re-emergence of your wonderful Jewish community. Thank you so much for your wonderful welcome and hospitality." I sat down to the community's thunderous applause.

The evening continued with more speeches, entertainment and food. At one point, there was a moment of interesting tension when an official from the town said in her speech that "the Torah was important not only for the Jewish community, but for the whole town as something of historical value." She then asked for it to be displayed in the town museum for a while.

Yacov Basin's reply was both swift and brilliantly incisive:

"If you would like to have such a valuable exhibit in the museum, you can appeal for help to the KGB. There are lots of such scrolls confiscated from Jews in the 1920's and 1930's in their depots."

My sister and myself agreed absolutely and Avril stood up and stated:

"This Torah was intended as a living spark for use by the Jewish community and not as a museum exhibit."

We did, however, agree, that the Torah could be displayed for just one day in the town museum on the condition that, at all times, it remained under Ludmila's watchful care.

Then Rabbi Abramovitch addressed the congregation talking about the significance of the Torah and explaining that though Baranovichi had no synagogue, a member of the community had lovingly built a beautiful ark for it.

He expressed the hope that this "Tree of Life," would inspire the community in its learning and said that he would endeavor to come from Minsk to teach and lead services as much as was possible.

Then the men and boys put on their tallits and the service began. It was meaningful and sweet, finishing with the youngsters leading the community in saying the blessings in Hebrew over the wine and challah.

As the Torah was carried through the crowded room first by the Rabbi and then by Bob and Jon, the community greeted it with enthusiasm and great emotion. With tears running down their faces, they reached out to touch and kiss it. It was obvious that its arrival was really important and had great significance for the Jews of Baranovichi, both young and old. With pride, my brother-in-law, Bob Brodey, carried the Torah to the Aron Kodesh.

A symbol of survival, regeneration and hope, this much-traveled Torah had been lovingly welcomed and was now was safely home again.

Notes:

Ivrit. The Hebrew language.

Tallit. Jewish fringed prayer shawl.

Aron Kodesh. The ark in a synagogue.

Challah. Braided bread traditionally baked to celebrate the Jewish Sabbath.

Draniki. Potato Latkes /Pancakes.

Bird Nests in the Skyhawk

I had always believed that flying was strictly for the birds so what was I doing walking out onto the hodgepodge airfield that was Pitt Meadows located twenty-eight miles outside Vancouver that sunny spring morning in 1992?

The truth was that I had been maneuvered into it by Abe, a friend I was visiting in this beautiful Canadian city. He had been bitten by the solo flying bug a year or so ago and now kept a small single engine plane based at Pitt Meadows.

The day before, sitting on the pebbly beach below his precariously cliff balanced summer cottage, we watched small planes land on waterskis in the bay. I had foolishly remarked, "Wow! That looks exciting."

The moment I uttered the words, I knew I was going to regret them and immediately tried to neutralize them with, "For some people."

It was too late. The opportunity had been created, it was just the opening Abe had been waiting for. There was no going back. I knew him.

"Yes," he agreed. "It's great. Why don't we take a short flight over Vancouver tomorrow? You'll love the views. I'll call Mike, the mechanic, and tell him to prepare Skyhawk 11."

Before I could say a word, he was gone, dashing up the steep path to the cottage to phone Mike to check the plane and weather and to arrange a flight plan. There was no stopping him.

I had sworn to my parents and Robert, my business partner, whom I had left to run our "China Ware House Company" store in Carnaby Street, that I would not do anything crazy like going up in a small single engine plane with an enthusiastic, but new and inexperienced pilot. Yet, here I was, a couple of days into my vacation and doing just that. Previously, I had overcome my flying fears with the justification that planes were huge and chock-full of modern technology, but this, by the sound of it, was going to be an engine on wings held together by string.

Thirty minutes later, Abe came bounding down the cliff path, a big grin on his face.

"It's all arranged. Our flight is tomorrow at 11:00 a.m. I've checked the weather and it's going to be a beautiful clear day with no clouds. You do want to come don't you?"

He threw this in as an afterthought, having of course already set everything up.

What was I going to say? *No way*? It wouldn't work. He was charming and persuasive and would not take no for an answer.

So here we were on a sunny Vancouver morning, walking across the grass field towards the tiny plane Abe had pointed out as his. He had filed a flight plan as soon as we arrived in the small control tower and was holding some navigation papers. He was wearing a well-worn brown leather flying jacket.

As we approached the Cessna 172, I could see a man, presumably Mike the mechanic, standing close to one of the wings. It had an open flap and Mike seemed to be pulling what appeared to be straw out of the wing.

"What's he doing?" I asked.

"Oh, it's bird nesting season," Abe replied cheerfully. "The birds really like the coziness of a small plane wing to build their nests. Mike's taking out the bird nests."

My mouth fell open.

"Bird nests?"

Suddenly, I had an image of Icarus and his wings coming unstuck. Icarus, feathers, wings and bird nests. Were we going to follow the same path? How could I get out of this?

Seeing the alarm etched on my face, Abe put a friendly arm around my shoulder.

"Vivien, it's really okay. All the pilots check their wings for bird nests at this time of the year. It's a well practiced safety measure."

Mike looked up and agreed.

"I'm finished. They are all out," he said, pointing to a pile of twigs and straw on the ground. "She's filled up and ready to go. It's a great day for a flight. Here, let me help you up."

He pulled a small crate up to the side of the plane and gave me a hand as I climbed aboard.

The cockpit was very small, just like the interior of a car but with a larger control panel and two seats in front and two behind. Abe climbed in the other side and pulled the door shut. There was no handle, just a piece of string.

"I'm just going to check some flight procedures. It won't take long." Putting on headphones, he began speaking to the control tower. For the next few minutes, he turned on and checked various switches and dials.

"We are almost ready to go," he said. " I have just got to give you the lowdown on some safety requirements." He rattled off a few instructions regarding safety, finishing with, "There's two parachutes on the back seat."

"Parachutes!" I exclaimed. "What are they doing back there? They should be strapped to our bodies. What are we supposed to do in an emergency, clamber over the seats and put them on while the plane is spiraling uncontrollably down towards earth?"

"Don't worry, Viv. Even if the engines lose power, I'm trained to glide Skyhawk down safely. Here's a sick bag in case you need it."

I looked at Abe, charming, but short. He was sitting on two cushions so he could see out. All this was hardly a confidence builder.

There were two conflicting conversations going on here. My inner voice was yelling,

Get out of here you idiot. It's dangerous. Run like mad.

However, my apparently calm exterior was replying to Abe's question, "Ready for take off?" with a voice that was definitely not mine, "Yes."

"Okay. Mike," Abe said leaning out of the cockpit. "Let's go."

Mike bent down and moved the wheel blocks, gave the propeller a couple of whirls and the engine hummed into life. He then gave a thumbs up and yelled, "Have a good flight."

Slowly and bumpily, we moved across the meadow past other small planes, mechanics and flying jackets. Then we were off the field and on a tarmac track that pretended to be a runway.

Abe cleared take off with the control tower and yelled above the engine, "Here we go!"

My stomach lurched and all the muscles in my body tensed. I clenched my teeth and closed my eyes and pushed my camera up against the window and started clicking. If I couldn't appreciate the flight now, perhaps at some future time (if there was going to be one) when my feet were firmly on the ground, I could enjoy the scenery.

There was a sense of speed, a rushing wind, and a sort of kick in the back as everything tilted upwards. My camera jerked, but I kept on taking photos with my teeth still clenched and my eyes shut. Somewhere in the distance above the noise of the engine, I heard a laugh and the sound of Abe's voice.

"Come on, Viv. Open your eyes. It's beautiful up here. We are as free as birds and there's nothing to be afraid of."

Gradually, I relaxed and found I was able to open my eyes. We were a couple of thousand feet up, flying above the airfield with its patchwork of Lilliputian figures and planes. Abe was confidently piloting us towards Vancouver Bay with its blue waters dotted with yachts, ferries and passenger ships.

"There's Lions Gate Bridge on the left," he shouted, tilting the plane.

"Don't do that," I yelled in alarm, hoping he was not going to loop the loop next.

The green gardens of Stanley Park came into view with glimpses of colorful totem poles. Then the streets, houses, and stores of Vancouver, Gastown and Granville Island. It really was beautiful circling the city and bay. Abe had just finished, talking to the control tower, when I said, "Thanks a lot Abe. This is great. I've actually enjoyed the flight, but I'm ready to go back now."

Abe turned towards me and I could see immediately he had something else in mind from the smile on his face.

"We can't."

"What do you mean we can't? You said, 'just a short flight around the bay' and we have now been flying for thirty minutes."

"Yes, but I have just checked out of Vancouver airspace and into a different control area. We are heading up the Fraser Valley for a spot of lunch."

I should have guessed. I was stuck up in the air with a novice flying enthusiast, eager to show off his newly acquired skills in a tiny toy airplane with no way of getting down to earth on my own. I was trapped.

"You exhibitionist!" I yelled. "You had this planned all the time didn't you?"

He laughed. " Oh come on Vivien, relax. This is the ultimate freedom. Go with it."

Did I have a choice? Was I a crocodile wimp or a spirited adventurer? This time I chose the latter. I put down my camera which had been clicking automatically all this time, and started to actually look, as we left behind the balconies and rooftops of Vancouver and proceeded to follow the course of a winding river.

Far below, birds floated up and down on streams of air and fields, orchards, barns and farms flashed by, framed by distant mountains. At certain points, logs being moved downstream, covered the surface of the Fraser River.

It really was spectacular. There was an incredible feeling of freedom with blue sky above and beautiful earth below. I was beginning to understand Abe's fascination with it. I melted into the experience, now beginning to love every minute of it.

As our flight continued, Abe yelled above the roar of the engines, "I'm just going to check the wind direction at Chilliwack Airport's landing field with the Fraser Valley air control. We should be arriving in about ten minutes."

The scenery continued to meander beautifully below as we flew like birds above it.

"There it is!" Abe pointed to what appeared to be a white handkerchief and small building in a curve of the river.

"That's our landing strip?"

Indeed it was. Abe was actually going to land the plane on that small space. My admiration for his newly acquired skills increased. However, I still found myself beginning to tense up again. *Stop!* I ordered myself. *This is a once-in-a-lifetime experience. Enjoy it. Don't close your eyes.*

And so with more than a little bravado, I forced myself to look as we came in to land, sliding in my seat as we began to descend. The river, trees and fields flashed by. The handkerchief grew larger and turned into a concrete strip. Then with a bump and a jolt we had landed.

"There's the pilot's clubhouse and restaurant," said Abe as the plane slowed and moved towards the building ahead. I could see tables and umbrellas on the outside veranda as we came to a stop directly in front of it.

Abe switched off the engine and the propeller slowed its windmill whirl. He undid his belt and mine and gave me a big hug. "Now wasn't that great?"

I hugged him back in agreement, glad we were safely back on firm ground.

"Let's go and get some lunch." He opened his door and jumped out, speaking to a mechanic who had come up to the plane to greet him.

"Hi Bill. Great day for a flight. Not a cloud in sight. This is Viv. We've popped in for lunch. Can you fill up Skyhawk for the return flight?"

"Sure," replied Bill. " Hi Viv. Did you enjoy the flight?"

"It was great," I said and actually meant it.

Abe came to my side of the plane and helped me down.

"Let's go. I'm starving."

As we walked the few steps into the clubhouse with Skyhawk parked just in front of it, I thought, *Wow this is the life. What a cool way to go to lunch. I really could get used to this.*

Even the flight back seemed something to look forward to.

The Chief Minister is in the Shower

Was this for real? I held my breath in amazement.
"Would you like his home phone number?"
"Excuse me, what did you say?" I asked, certain that I had misunderstood.
"Would you like his home phone number? You seem to keep missing him," repeated Glenda, his Personal Assistant.
Did I want his home phone number? Was she serious? Of course I did! The home number in question was that of the Chief Minister of The British Virgin Islands. I had been trying to reach him for several weeks to discuss an official project for the U.K. division of The International Chamber of Commerce that I was working on in London for a publishing and internet company.
"Yes please," I answered. "That will be extremely helpful."
I quickly wrote down the number she gave me, repeating it clearly to make sure I had gotten it right.
"Will it be alright for me to call now?"

"Well, I would wait about an hour to give him time to reach home. He has just left the building," replied the ever-helpful Glenda.

"Thank you very much for all your help. Have a good evening," I said as I ended the call.

For the next hour, my fingers hovered above the phone, itching to make the call. The project involved a new website for Global Offshore Centers for investors from around the world. Its focus was going to be the emerging Caribbean countries who were enthusiastically developing this area of business, rather than the arrogant and jaded older established regions in Europe. The idea was to showcase the offshore facilities offered to investors by the following nine countries: British Virgin Islands, Commonwealth of Dominica, St. Kitts and Nevis, St. Vincent and The Grenadines, Turks and Caicos Islands, Belize, Anguilla, Grenada and The Bahamas. It was a challenging project and the only hope of getting it off the ground was to make a presentation at the Chief Minister and government minister levels. Not an easy task, but nevertheless a fascinating challenge to work outside the normal boundaries of presentation.

Here goes, I muttered to myself picking up the phone. *Let's see what happens. I'll probably get some flunky who will take a message and forget all about it.*

I could hear the phone ringing a few times all those sunny miles away. Then it was picked up and a pleasant and friendly voice said, "Good Evening."

"Good evening," I replied, and quickly introduced myself. "My name is Vivien Stephens and I am calling on behalf of the U.K. division of The International Chamber of Commerce. I wonder if it would be convenient for me to speak to the Chief Minister regarding an important new global offshore center initiative?"

Keep it brief, keep it brief, my head instructed my mouth, well aware that these first two minutes of conversation were crucial to any future progress.

"Can you call back a little later?" the pleasant voice replied. "My husband is taking a shower at the moment."

"Certainly. I'll call back again in about thirty minutes. Thank you."

I put the phone down, hardly able to contain my delight. What an unexpected and surprising response. The norm, when trying to present a new project, was to be blocked by mid-management ego, and vice-presidents inflated by their own importance. How refreshing to get such a wonderful natural response without pomp and circumstance! *The Chief Minister was taking a shower.* How delightfully normal. I loved it.

When he answered the phone some thirty minutes later, the Chief Minister was courteous and to the point. I explained the initiative and the other countries in the Caribbean region who would be featured on the website.

"Would you send full details to my office and then contact Glenda, my personal assistant, to set a time when we can discuss this further next week?" he requested. He then ended the conversation with a pleasant, "Have a good evening."

Following further discussions regarding the specifics of the project, on March 14, 2001, I received an email from The Chief Minister confirming the participation of The British Virgin Islands on the website.

Several months later, following a vacation with family and friends, enjoying as always the beauty and buzz of San Francisco and the Bay Area, I returned to my office in London.

"Welcome back, Vivien. How was your vacation?" asked Mark, the floor manager.

"Great and, as usual, over much too quickly," I responded.

"Oh, by the way, while you were on holiday some bloke came here to see you. I think he was a minister from somewhere in the Caribbean. He just turned up with an assistant. No one was expecting him or knew who he was. Maurice took care of him."

"What!" I exclaimed." I didn't have any appointments with any minister or anyone else for that matter. Why would I make an appointment if I was going to be out of the office?"

I rushed to turn on my computer to see if there could be any explanation for this strange and unexpected occurrence. Logging on, I ran my eye down a month's accumulated emails looking for something that might explain what had happened. Scrolling down, I found the culprit. Dated June 14, 2001, it had been sent from Glenda's personal email with an address that looked more like spam than an official announcement and it had gone straight into my email, bypassing the main office completely.

Opening the email, I read the following announcement:

<u>Formal Visit to London by Chief Minister,
The Honorable Ralph T. O'Neal</u>

"With reference to the above captioned, please be advised that the Honorable Ralph T. O'Neal, Chief Minister of the British Virgin Islands is expected to be in London from 20th-28th June, 2001, and would wish to meet with the manager along with yourself on the morning of 27th June.

Please advise soonest what time would be most convenient to conduct the meeting.

I look forward to hearing from you soon."
Glenda Wilson
Personal Assistant to the Chief Minister.

I stared at the screen aghast. I had been out of the office for the month of June and had no idea of this impending visit. What must the Chief Minister have thought, turning up with no one expecting him, no reception party?

Surely, my head was going to be on the chopping block for this.

There was nothing else for it. I had to go and see the boss and eat humble pie for this embarrassing mix up.

Steeling myself, I knocked on the door of Maurice, the publisher and owner of the company.

He greeted me with a grin, "What you been up to? Good vacation?"

"Yes, thank you," I stuttered, "but what about the visit of the Chief Minister of The British Virgin Islands? I've just seen the email from his personal assistant and understand that he just turned up in the office and no one knew he was coming or even knew who he was."

Maurice roared with laughter, "Yeah, there was a bit of a mix up at first, but don't worry, we soon sorted it out. I explained you were away on vacation and we spent an enjoyable afternoon drinking whisky and discussing cricket. Everything was fine in the end."

Not completely convinced, I decided to get on the phone to make apologies and explanations to Glenda about the mix up. Listening for a few minutes, she also laughed as she interrupted me, "Don't worry Vivien. The Chief Minister enjoyed his visit to your office. Apparently, he had a great time discussing cricket with somebody."

Thank goodness for cricket, I thought as I put down the phone, *the trustworthy and solid backbone of England. What would we do without it?*

Whitewater Rafting in Costa Rica
May 2011

The Rio Sarapiqui appeared gentle and friendly as we splashed aboard the blue rubber raft, looking like five ladybirds with our orange lifejackets and safety helmets. We clasped our short red and yellow paddles as we waited for directions from our muscular stubble-cheeked Costa Rican instructor.

With a "right paddle, left paddle," we were off, floating on the current of the gently flowing pebbly river. The rainforest, with its multitude of colorful birds constantly landing by the riverside and chattering monkeys swinging from branch to branch, was a delight for city eyes.

"This is the life," proclaimed Virginia, looking up at the blue sky at a pair of toucans flying overhead.

"What's that noise?" asked Carol, as an audible roar began to build.

It grew louder and louder as the raft began to bob and bounce and the friendly river started to swirl and snarl.

"Hold tight everyone," yelled Javier, our instructor, "there's a few rocks and a small drop in the river up ahead."

Nothing like understatement! It appeared we were approaching some fast running rapids.

"Brace yourselves," shouted Javier, as a plume of foaming water lifted us up and swirled us around and tossed us like a discarded cork, back and forth.

Adrenalin flowed. It was both terrifying and exhilarating as we gave up all attempts at paddling and just shrieked and held on to the side of the raft, watching the raging water and flying foam splash over the side and soak us. We zigzagged along, somehow managing to stay in the raft and not be thrown out.

Then, as suddenly as it had started, the roaring subsided and we were in calm flowing waters again. The river was once more our gently embracing friend.

Volcanoes, Trains and Ocean Liners

St. Lucia.

The air was heavy with sulphur. It was December, 2013, and I was wedged in the half open door of a minibus, momentarily stopped on a bridge. Far below us, a couple covered from head to toe in volcanic mud, was indulging in dabbing mud tattoos on each other, making them look like skeletons. To my left, white smoke was billowing from a group of rocks. I was snapping furiously with my camera trying to capture the scene. I really wanted to get out of the bus in order to more readily absorb the atmosphere of the Soufriere drive-in volcano located on St. Lucia between its two impressive Piton Mountains.

However, as soon as I had started to climb down, our guide had shouted, "Everyone stay on the bus! This is not an official stop, but a photo opportunity."

Suddenly, a deep voice close to my ear said, "Why don't you just get out? We won't leave you behind."

I looked round in surprise, as the bearded man behind me, repeated the statement adding somewhat more urgently, "Go on. Why don't you just get off? Go on do it!"

It was Dwayne, a dairy farmer from West Virginia, and a fellow traveler from my cruise ship. Had I *offended him in some way that he was encouraging me to get off, just as the driver was obviously about to leave? Perhaps my English accent had irritated him?*

Much as I wanted to get out, I wasn't looking to be stranded in the middle of these still very active volcanic springs.

"No, I'm good. I've got all the photos I want," I said, moving away from the door and back to my seat next to Jon. As I went past him, Dwayne looked really upset.

St. Kitts.

The air the next day was very different, fresh and sparkling like white wine, as we sat on the open deck of a steam train traveling around the island of St. Kitts. This single-track railway had previously served the sugar cane industry. Now, in splendid retirement, it chugged along at a leisurely pace, showing visitors the glorious landscape of this lush island. We steamed past villages, back gardens and brilliant turquoise bays with white sand fringed with palm trees and up into the thick green foliage of rainforests along the way crossing high trestle bridges. It was a delicious mix of elegance and nature, as we sipped piña coladas and reached out for waving palm fronds.

After a while, I started chatting with a fellow traveler who had been born in Kenya, but now lived in West Virginia with her software engineer husband. I explained that though I now lived in San Francisco, I was originally from London.

"But I lived in London for several years. That's where I met my husband," she exclaimed.

"Where did you live?"

"Newham, what about you?"

"Hackney."

These two London boroughs adjoin each other, so it appeared we had almost been neighbors in England, but only got to actually meet halfway across the world, here on the island of St. Kitts.

At that moment, Dwayne suddenly appeared from an adjoining carriage. He greeted us cheerfully. However, I immediately started to wonder if he was going to encourage me to jump off the train on one of its stops? Perhaps he was considering giving me a friendly push? But he just stood there silently.

I decided to take the initiative and said, "I think you should meet a fellow West Virginian," introducing him to the Kenyan woman.

Suddenly, there was a shrill whistle as the train approached a high trestle bridge. I decided to move as far away from him as possible so as not to tempt fate. I left the two of them chatting and rejoined Jon for another piña colada.

The Cruise Ship.
It was a few days later and I was standing on deck enjoying the cool evening breeze. Tomorrow we were due to dock in Puerto Rico at the end of our cruise. For once, I was elegantly attired, in a long black velvet skirt topped by a turquoise silk blouse. I was holding onto the deck rail as I was balanced, somewhat precariously, on five-inch stiletto heels. The captain's farewell dinner was due to start in the main restaurant in a little while and having monopolized the shower for longer than usual, I had decided to give Jon some space to shave and dress.

Earlier that evening, we had watched the sun set in a blaze of brilliant pinks and oranges, its afterglow an artist's palette of changing tones and shapes. Now the night sky glowed, illuminated by twinkling stars and a bright full moon. In the distance, a small island appeared to be gliding past as the waves gently splashed against the silently moving ship.

I had deliberately chosen an isolated deck away from the hustle and bustle of the ship and I was standing in the area close to where a dozen lifeboats were silently suspended on long chains. Relaxing after a hectic day of exploration on the island of St. Martin, I closed my eyes enjoying the gentle motion and sheer calm of the evening.

Suddenly, the silence was broken by a creaking noise. I looked round.

Was one of the lifeboats moving? Was that a light that flashed from green to amber?

No, everything was still; it must have been my imagination.
I turned back to gaze at the horizon and to listen to the sound of the lapping waves.

Once again, there was a creaking sound. I spun round quickly and this time it was not my imagination. The same lifeboat was swinging wildly and a small light above the lifeboat briefly flashed from green to amber to red. I stood there staring at it, wondering what was happening and, as I did so, a hand appeared and made a grab for one of the supporting chains. As I watched mesmerized, a dark figure suddenly pulled himself up. As the lifeboat swayed dangerously, he hooked his leg around the chain and started sliding down towards the deck. He was dressed in black jeans with a black T-shirt. As he emerged from the shadows onto the moonlit deck, I saw that his hair and beard looked unkempt and his eyes had a glazed look to them. I looked again and then, with a shock of recognition, realized that it was Dwayne. *What was it with this guy?*

As he moved towards me, I felt myself edging back, only to find myself right up against the deck rail. I could move no further. Looking along the length of the deck, I realized there was no one around. After all, wasn't that what I had wanted?

"Hello, I've been waiting for you. Don't be afraid," Dwayne said, as he drew close. "I knew you would come."

His face was smeared with dirt, like a camouflage disguise and his breath smelt of beer. He put his hand on my back. "I knew if I waited long enough, you would be here. After all, you enjoy escaping just like me. Now's the perfect time. Look the sea is calm, and we can jump overboard and swim to that island. We can be happy there."

I looked at him in bewilderment. Was he drunk and joking? What was this thing he had about getting off moving buses, trains and now boats?

My bewilderment turned to horror as he climbed up on to the rail, grabbed my arm and started to pull me towards him.

"Look it's easy. I'll show you. We just have to jump. It'll be fine."

Terrified by what was happening and stalling for time, I found myself calmly saying, "No, that's not a good idea. My long skirt will make it difficult to swim and I have to have my Jimmy Choo stilettos if you want me to be happy on that island so let's use one of the lifeboats instead."

To my astonishment, he grinned, jumped off the rail and said, "Good thinking. Let's get started."

He grabbed hold of the chain and started to climb up and back into the lifeboat. As he did so, there was a flash of light, as a spotlight focused on the lifeboat and a loud voice boomed, "This is the captain speaking. Come down from that lifeboat immediately Dwayne and nobody will get hurt."

Shaken, I looked down the deck to see six ship's officers running towards us. What was going to happen now?

Dwayne reached down into the lifeboat and held up his hand. He was holding a can of beer.

"Okay. I'll come quietly," he yelled. "It was only a joke."

As he clambered down the chain with the beer in his back pocket, he winked at me. One of the officers grabbed and handcuffed him. Another came up to me asking, "Are you okay?"

"Yes. I'm fine now that it's over," I said "But what was that all about? Who is he really? You seem to know him."

"Yes, we do. He is a paying passenger. Every time he comes aboard, he assumes a different character: a farmer, lawyer or a businessman, but he is actually an out-of-work actor who is trying to write a screenplay for an action film and just can't find the right ending so he keeps acting out these ridiculous docudramas. He was warned the last time that he would be banned from future cruises if he continued his antics, so I guess this time he has really done it. Anyway, let me see you back to your cabin."

As I entered our cabin, I heard a muffled sound that seemed to get louder and louder rising to an urgent crescendo. A voice seemed to be saying something over and over again. Gradually it became clearer.

"Vivien. Vivien wake up! We are going to be late."

I opened my eyes and, standing in front of me was Jon, looking smart in his tux. I was fully dressed in a long black velvet skirt topped by a turquoise silk blouse. I must have dozed off while waiting for him to finish in the shower. We had, after all, spent an energetic day exploring beautiful St. Martin.

"Okay I'm ready," I said, reaching down for my sparkly Bernie Mev shoes.

As I put them on I said, "I've just had this really strange dream."

"Come on let's go," said Jon impatiently. "You can tell me all about your dream later. We are supposed to be meeting Dwayne and his wife in the lounge near the restaurant at 7:00 p.m. for drinks and it's nearly that time now. It's the last night of the cruise before docking in Puerto Rico and we don't want to be late for the captain's dinner, do we?"

Almost Worth Breaking an Arm For

He was leaning dangerously over the balcony rail, waving frantically with his one good arm. Fresh-faced with blond hair, he was wearing a red sweater and was twelve years old. His other arm was held tight by a white sling. He seemed to be shouting something as his good arm waved furiously to catch my attention.

I was standing below in the casino hall, feeding ten-cent coins into a hungry slot machine. The jangle of falling coins from the surrounding slots, together with the sound of people chatting and background music made it impossible for me to hear him, so I waved back, smiled reassuringly and continued playing.

As the coins clinked and clattered, I thought how the weekend had begun very differently. It was February, 1988, and I was on a winter holiday break from London, visiting Avril and Bob and their family in San Francisco. We had decided to take a few days skiing and snow walking in Squaw Valley.

The snow was thick on the ground when we arrived and my nephews, Daniel and Thomas, were raring to go. They were to ski on the upper slopes with Bob and his friend Gilles, both skilled skiers, while Avril and I were to stay lower down the mountain and try cross-country snow walking.

With a "See you later," we went our separate ways.

We soon arrived at the lower snow meadows and Avril put on her cross-country skis. With a look of determination on her face, she grasped her walking poles and said, "Here we go," and took off.

I was left to start more cautiously. As soon as I began to move, I knew that I was in for a challenging day. My feet immediately appeared to be in conflict, pulling, slipping and sliding in different directions.

"It's easy, you'll enjoy it," Avril had said earlier that morning.

"Are you sure?" I had asked dubiously, remembering my one miserable attempt at ice skating years ago when I was a student at Sussex University. On that occasion, I had given up counting after falling twenty-nine times in the first hour.

"Come on, don't be chicken," she had taunted.

"Okay. I'll give it a try," I said rising to the bait. "It can't be any worse than the ice skating."

However, a couple of hours later, as I landed with a thump on the icy path for the umpteenth time and struggled to keep my balance and avoid crashing into ever approaching menacing trees, I realized that I was really not enjoying this at all. But we were here for another day. *How was I going to get out of this tomorrow?*

The answer came from an unexpected source. As we walked from the aerial tram to meet Bob and the boys later that afternoon, we saw them emerging from the first aid medical room. Daniel, my eldest nephew had his arm in a sling. He had taken a nasty fall on an icy patch and fractured his arm. There was to be no more skiing for him this trip.

"It's not fair," he said, as we sat in our ski gear drinking hot chocolate on an outside restaurant deck, surrounded by a clear blue sky and a ring of snow capped peaks.

"You are all going to be having fun tomorrow skiing. What am I going to do?"

"Well we can come up here on the aerial tram and watch everybody," said Avril. "I'll stay with you."

"Fat lot of good that will be," replied Daniel kicking the bench in frustration.

I had found my opt out for tomorrow.

"I've an idea," I said coming to the rescue. "It's just going to make you feel more angry watching everyone have a good time. How would you like to go to Reno instead? I hear there's a good show at the Circus Circus Casino and you can eat all the food you want in their restaurant buffet. Also, if I get to play the slots, I'll split my winnings with you. How does that sound?"

"Thanks. That sounds much better than hanging around here like an idiot doing nothing," he replied.

Early the next day, we caught the Greyhound bus from Truckee where we were staying and headed for Reno. Daniel was somewhat subdued, his arm was aching and he was still upset at missing the day skiing. However, as we entered the bright lights and noise of Circus Circus, he began to look more cheerful.

I noticed the first real spark of interest as we stood on an escalator when this precocious twelve-year-old started gazing at the short skirts and legs of the pretty young waitresses standing ahead of him.

"That's cool," he muttered.

"What's that you're looking at Daniel?' I asked, teasing him.

"Nothing, just things," he answered, blushing a deep red.

As we walked into the buffet restaurant for lunch with its counters piled high with mouth-watering food, his eyes lit up. He saw the pizza, pancakes, French fries, mac and cheese, fried chicken, waffles and calorie busting desserts. For the first time that day, I saw a big smile. He tucked into the food with relish and grinned as we finished our meal.

"Let's go and look at the acrobats and trapeze artists," I suggested.

We stood on the balcony watching the acrobats jumping and tumbling and the trapeze artists flying gracefully from perch to swing under the high tent-like roof. Below the huge safety net, the rows and rows of slots and blackjack and roulette tables were another world.

"You said you would share your winnings with me if you played the slot machines," Daniel reminded me after a while.

"Okay." I replied. "But children are not allowed on the main casino floor. You will have to stay here on the balcony and not move. I'll find some slots where you can watch me."

"I can do that," he agreed.

Once on the casino floor, I got some rolls of coins, slipped them into my jacket pocket, found a slot machine in Daniel's sight line and started playing. Taking coins from my right hand pocket, in line with my rule of never gambling my winnings, I dropped any coins that plopped out of the machine in my left hand winning pocket. Since he was to share in the winnings, I couldn't understand why Daniel was still waving frantically at me and beckoning me back.

Soon enough, I'd used all my playing coins, and went to rejoin Daniel on the balcony. As soon as he saw me approaching he started to walk away from me. I rushed to catch up with him.

"What's the matter?" I asked.

He stared back at me angrily and said nothing.

"What's the matter?" I repeated.

"You lost all our winnings!" he shouted at me. "You said that you would share them with me and you went and lost them."

"No I didn't," I replied.

"Yes you did. I saw you put all the coins into the machine," he patted the right hand pocket of my jacket where he had seen me put the rolls of coins. "Look, it's empty, there's nothing left."

At last I understood. I realized that the angle I had been standing had blocked the view of my left hand winning pocket so from his point of view his assumption was right.

"No, I definitely did not lose your winnings," I stated firmly.

"Where are they then?" he asked.

"How about here," I laughed, pointing to my winning pocket. "Put your hand in this pocket and see what's there."

He pulled out a handful of coins and put them on a nearby coffee table.

"There's more," I said, as he pulled out the rest of the coins.

His expression changed.

"Now count them up and you can have half as agreed," I said.

I had played twenty dollars worth of coins and was interested to see how much I had lost. For the next few minutes, Daniel concentrated on separating and counting the pile of coins. He finished triumphantly saying, "There's eight dollars and ten cents for you, and eight dollars ten cents for me. Thanks Viv."

The smile was back on his face.

"Do you have room for an ice cream before we go and catch the bus back to Truckee?" I asked.

"Yes please," he replied with a grin.

As we slurped our giant ice cream cones on the way out of Circus Circus, Daniel suddenly stopped and planted a sticky kiss on my cheek and then said, "Thanks for bringing me here Viv. It was fun. You know all this was almost worth breaking my arm for."

Michelin Boy

"Morning Viv," said my ten-year-old nephew, Thomas, sitting up in bed excitedly. "I'm ready for breakfast and Disney World. Let's go."

"Just a minute. Hold on," I replied as I pulled back the hotel curtains. "Have a shower first and then breakfast."

I turned round to face him and immediately did a double take. *Who was this?*

This mini Michelin man bouncing on the bed, this balloon of a boy with a puffy face, a nose twice its normal size and a deep set pinholes of eyes that had almost disappeared. This was not the fresh-faced, rosy-cheeked, curly-haired boy I had arrived with in Florida yesterday afternoon.

What had happened? Where had he gone?

It had been a hectic few days. Perhaps I was hallucinating? Was I exhausted from the long flight from London to San Francisco to collect Thomas, leaving almost immediately to fly back eastward to Florida to deliver on a yearlong promise to take him to Disney World?

Panic started to set in. *What was I to do?* I was responsible for him.

How would my sister and brother-in-law respond if I returned to California with this blown up monster instead of the normal sweet-faced boy they had entrusted to my care? It was June, 1989, and I was an English visitor to America, totally unprepared for this, and I didn't have a clue what to do.

Calm down. Stop panicking you idiot, I admonished myself. *Stop and think.*

"Are you feeling ill?" I asked Thomas.

"No, I'm feeling fine," replied my nephew sounding puzzled. "Why are you asking? Let's get going we're wasting time."

"Come with me. I want to show you something, but don't get frightened," I said.

"Frightened? I'm never frightened," he answered with all the bravado of a ten-year-old now looking really baffled.

I led him to the bathroom and stood him in front of the mirror.

"Wow! Cool! Who's that?"

Then looking a little closer he said, "Is that me? I do look a bit funny."

"Has this ever happened before?" I asked trying to think a bit more rationally, but at the same time wondering what I could have exposed him to that would cause such an alarming transformation in such a short time.

"Well, I'm allergic to cats and they sometimes give me a rash and there were some cats when we visited Bob's sister in Carmel the other day."

Allergy! At last I had something I could understand, something to grasp onto.

"Are you sure you are feeling okay?"

"Yes, I'm fine. Let's go."

"Sit there a moment," I ordered pointing to a chair and made a grab for the phone and called the Radisson Hotel reception.

"Can you please help me? I have a ten-year-old boy who has swelled up overnight. Where is the nearest medical center?"

The receptionist must have heard the panic in my voice because he cut in and said, "Don't worry ma'am, we have a doctor available close by. I'll give him a call and he will be with you immediately."

Twenty minutes later, there was a knock on the door.

"I'm Dr. Sinclair," the man announced as I opened the door. "I hear you have a problem." He walked into the room and stared intently at Thomas. "Well, he is somewhat swollen. Let me examine him and see what's going on."

"He's been near cats and is apparently allergic to them," I offered in explanation.

"Now young man what have you been up to?" Dr. Sinclair directed the question to Thomas as he began to examine him.

"Well, we just arrived yesterday afternoon and I have been swimming in the pool."

"Ah!" said the doctor. "How do you feel? Do you have a headache or feel sick?"

"No," replied my nephew. "I feel fine."

"What about an upset stomach?"

"I really feel okay I hope this is not going to stop me going to Disney World, Universal Studios and the Kennedy Space Center."

Dr. Sinclair turned to me and said, "This appears to be an allergic reaction to the mixing of cats, swimming pool chemicals and heat. I'll prescribe a week's steroid course which should bring the swelling down. He is definitely not infectious and, as long as he feels up to it, you can finish your visit as planned."

"Thank you, thank you," I said.

He must have seen the relief in my eyes at the confirmation that I had not somehow been the cause of permanent damage to my young nephew.

"Where can I find a pharmacy nearby?" I asked.

"Come with me," he replied.

Turning to Thomas, he smiled. "Good-bye young man. Remember to stay away from cats and too much sun. Enjoy yourself."

I followed him along the corridor as he left and into the elevator.

Parked in front of the hotel was a large car. He unlocked the boot and revealed what appeared to be a miniature pharmacy, row upon row of bottles and pills.

"Here you are," he said, handing me the steroids. "This should bring down the swelling. He'll be back to normal in a few days. Don't worry."

I gave him my Visa card, which he processed, and asked for the relevant paper work to give to my sister's medical plan and thanked him again. This guy was a marvel, a walking surgery, pharmacy and bank all rolled into one– nothing like what I was used to in the United Kingdom.

Earlier that year, while in the planning stage of my upcoming spring visit to America, Thomas had written to me saying, "I read your letter and I almost jumped for joy at the thrill of going to Disney World," and *jumping for joy* was exactly what I felt like doing as I rushed back to our room. I was now feeling normal for the first time that morning, incredibly relieved that this was just an allergic blip to our adventure rather than a major disaster.

An hour later after breakfast and after calling my sister in San Francisco to explain what had happened, we were waiting at the hotel reception for the Kissimmee shuttle bus to take us to Disney World, that magic kingdom for children of all ages.

The week sped by in a mixture of fun and enjoyment at The Magic Kingdom, Universal Studios, Sea World and the Kennedy Space Center. Everything was as interesting and entertaining as we had anticipated with one amazing and unexpected bonus.

Thomas felt fine; however looking as he did, a cross between an inflated balloon and a Michelin man, we didn't have to line up for anything. As soon as we approached a ride, people took one look at him and hurriedly rushed away. It saved us hours of waiting and standing in line.

Ironically, we arrived back in San Francisco on the last day of his steroid course and he had almost returned to his normal rosy-cheeked self.

"What was all the panic about?" asked my sister as she met us in the arrival hall. "Where's the Michelin boy?"

"I've photos to prove it," I replied defensively. "You'll see!"

Interestingly, years later in a college English class, Thomas rated "The Michelin Boy Trip," as one of his most enjoyable vacations.

Me? I remember it as one of my most delightful, but stressful travel experiences.

Are You Ready For The Next Adventure?

"Well, are you ready for the next adventure?" I asked, looking at my eighty-nine-year-old mother with her natural jet-black hair and smooth unwrinkled complexion. She gazed back at me with her lower lip quivering slightly and, in her quiet voice, she said, "Yes."

I held her hand feeling the outline of the arthritic bumps on her warm fingers as we took one last look around our family home with its empty rooms. Stripped clean by our shippers, it now felt like neutralized and impersonal space.

Yet, as we slowly wandered through the rooms for the last time, memories started to lurch from every nook and cranny, floodlit by sunlight streaming in through the curtainless bay windows.

Bedrooms with sweet recollections of childhood goodnight kisses and hugs brought to mind my father's prickly moustache and the delicious scent of my mother's face powder.

The kitchen with its comfortable cozy lunches around the round oak table and the enchanting perfume of my father's roses wafting in from the garden to mix with the smell of my mother's freshly baked apple strudel.

Friday night and the warm glow of flickering light as my mother lit the Shabbat candles and my father chanted the Shabbat blessings over the sweet spicy wine and the poppy seeded challah.

The noise and laughter and animated discussions of those wonderful family gatherings, of grandparents, aunts, uncles and cousins enjoying my mother's chicken and kneidel soup and tasty casseroles. The memory was so vivid that I wanted to reach out and grab one of her famed roast potatoes.

But suddenly the room was thrown into shadow as the sun disappeared behind some grey clouds. The memories flickered for a moment, as if waving goodbye, and then disappeared.

"Let's go," I said.

My mother, with her head held high, took her cane and said, "Yes, let's go," ready to embark on a new adventure at an age when most people just want to stay put. I slammed the door shut behind us and we walked towards the taxi and our new lives in a faraway land.

"We're here," I said six weeks later on June 20, 2005, as we walked into the empty, but freshly painted rooms of a ranch style house on the other side of the world. The California sunlight streamed in from all directions, sparkling diamonds on the nearby Pacific Ocean and brushing the surrounding hills with gold. The rooms looked friendly but bare.

"What do you think?" I asked my mother as my brother-in-law Bob and my sister, Avril wandered around the house. My nephews and great-nephews were playing catch in the garden.

"It's lovely now being close to the family and being able to spend time with the grandchildren and great-grandchildren. Much better than just talking on the phone. The house will be fine when we unpack our things and personalize it," she replied smiling, looking summery in a bright flowered dress.

And so it was. Our container arrived the same day that we got the keys to our new house and within a few weeks, when we had personalized it with all our familiar clutter–the ornaments, paintings and photos and the welcoming aroma of home cooking— it seemed as if the memories had found new nooks and crannies and, once again, we were home.

Chicken Soup, Poppadoms and Succotash

"Well, I guess this is it," said Spencer easing his large frame out of the yellow taxi.

I followed him out onto the station forecourt and was immediately engulfed in the all-embracing safety of his bear like hug. My face disappeared into the folds of his checkered shirt as my arms struggled to embrace just about half of his rotund circumference. It was September 17, 2009, and the moment I had been both looking forward to, yet dreading for weeks. My safe bubble was about to dissolve.

The morning had begun in the manner that I had come to regard as normal with Raj hooting in friendly greeting at 9:30 a.m. Shutting the front door, I clambered aboard the yellow taxi to be welcomed by Raj's cheerful, "Good Morning."

Spencer gave me an easygoing smile as he moved to make room for me on the back seat eagerly asking,

"Well, how was it?"

"Tasty and delicious," I replied. "Thanks."

The "it" was Spencer's comfort gift to me, a favorite okra succotash recipe with spicy Cajun seasoning that held sweet sunny memories of his childhood in Louisiana playing in the fields, climbing trees and jumping into natural pools with youthful bravado, ignoring the alligator warning signs. It held precious memories of family picnics and barbeques with steaming bowls of succotash, barbequed chicken and tasty grilled alligator steaks.

It was a remembered world so very different from his life today as a retired engineer, a widower living in San Francisco, enjoying frequent visits with his two grandchildren in the East Bay.

As the taxi picked up speed and left the morning mists of Pacifica, heading towards the clearer skies of South San Francisco, I thought of my comfort gift to him. The chicken and kneidel soup recipe with its equally vivid and precious childhood recollections. The warmth and laughter of our family around the dining table in London on cold winter nights, savoring my mother's tasty chicken soup and wonderful cannon ball kneidels (dumplings), followed by casseroled chicken and crispy roast potatoes and steaming apple pie made from tart Granny Smith apples. The safety and security of those family gatherings that we took for granted and thought would last forever.

Now, half a world away, I was living in Pacifica and enjoying the natural beauty of California's coastline and the vitality and charm of nearby San Francisco; however, just the mention of chicken soup and kneidels, was enough to instantly evoke those magic moments.

"Was it as good as my curry and poppadoms?" asked Raj, interrupting my train of thought.

"They were both delicious," I replied, "but in different ways."

Spencer nodded in agreement.

It was Raj who had first provided us with the idea of food, five weeks ago, as a precious gift of distraction when our three musketeers journey had begun. Intuitively, he had sensed a need to keep us occupied and interested during the daily half hour rides.

Raj had teased our taste buds with the flavors of India, garam masala, cumin, coriander, turmeric and chili powder–spices that gave exotic fire and character to vegetables and rice–accompanied by crispy, crunchy poppadoms. For him, the flavors evoked warm memories of his home village in the State of Gujarat where his mother cooked flavorful dishes for him and his brothers and sisters. Now he was living in San Bruno with his wife and two children, working all hours building his new taxi business. He regularly spoke with his family in India on Skype.

"We are almost here," said Raj, as the taxi turned into the hi-tech park at Oyster Point with its numerous new biotech buildings silhouetted against the sky. In the adjoining park, boats bobbed up and down in the marina on the bay and a pod of pelicans flew overhead in amazing synchronized flight.

I stared out of the window, surprised as usual, that the journey had been so enjoyable and quick. Raj drove through the parking lot and up to the entrance of the new state-of-the-art Kaiser Permanente Radiation Oncology Center and we got out. "I'm off to collect somebody else, but I'll be back by the time you both finish. See you soon," said Raj, driving off.

Spencer held the door for me and we went to check in for our respective treatments.

"It's your last treatment day today," smiled the friendly receptionist as I walked to robe up for the last of my two-minute radiation sessions for breast cancer.

I felt elated that I had reached this point, but also somewhat sad. For these past five weeks, I had been in a safe cocooned environment with friendly and understanding medical staff and, more importantly, I had bonded with the other patients undergoing treatment. They had become familiar faces and we had connected through the shared experience of battling unexpected trauma. Now this safe bubble was about to disappear.

"I must go," said Spencer, bringing me back to the present. He released me from his enormous hug. "I have another two weeks of treatment and I am really going to miss our morning rides. All the best to you."

"And you too, Spencer. Take care," I said as I watched him walk towards the Bart station entrance and disappear.

Goodbye my friend, I thought struggling to make sense of my ambiguous feelings. I was sad to see him go, but hoping that we would never have to make this particular journey together again.

"Get in, Vivien and I'll drive you home," said Raj. "Cheer up. It's a great day. Your treatment's finished."

"It sure is," I smiled. "Life's good, let's go."

Pink Nails

It had been a long day and my eyes were beginning to close. It was the evening of June 3, 2014, and midnight was fast approaching.

Earlier in the day, I had walked a mile or so to a local school where I had voted in just my second election as a still relatively new American citizen. I had then navigated the journey from Pacifica to the Sunset District on public transportation with a Muni sickout in progress, but still arrived in time for the start of Shavuot celebrations at Ner Tamid Synagogue. It was to be an evening of study to celebrate the giving of the Torah on Mount Sinai.

Four communities in San Francisco had come together to celebrate the festival, Ner Tamid, Or Shalom, Beth Israel Judea and B'nai Emunah. The evening had started with a wine and cheese welcome, followed by a series of offbeat lectures:

"Dust in the Wind," by Rabbi Mark Melamut.
"Blintzes and Blasphemy," by Rabbi Moshe Levin.
"Betraying Perfection," by Rabbi Katie Mizrachi.
"Cheesecake in Paradise," by Rabbi Danny Gottlieb.

To keep us fired up, we had paused half way through the program for a potluck dairy dessert, featuring at least a dozen different types of mouthwatering cheesecakes.

Now weighed down by calorie overload, the result of unrestrained indulgence in sampling too many delicious flavors of cheesecake and wine, my drooping eyelids had taken on a will of their own. Desperate not to fall asleep for the closing program, "Experiencing Mount Sinai," I looked around frantically for a distraction to keep me awake. Rows of heads and handout notes came into my roving gaze. No help there. I looked around again and suddenly a flash of bright audacious pink caught my eye. A definite statement of intent. My eye was drawn to it like a magnet.

It was bright pink nail varnish and adorned the hands of a women sitting next to me. Her hands were those of an older woman, veined, full of character and beautifully manicured. They were lit up by this blaze of pink, an eloquent statement proclaiming, *I might be aging, but this is who I still am!*

Looking up, I suddenly realized how well these hands suited their owner. They belonged to Mira Shelub, born in Zhetel, a small town in eastern Poland, now Belarus.

She had escaped from a labor camp with two Jewish partisans and had been a forest dwelling resistance fighter during World War II. She had fought with the Jewish partisans in the forests of Belarus for two and a half years. Her strong will, determination and defiance kept her alive to survive the war. Marrying a fellow partisan, she had come to America and raised a family. Today, in her nineties, she bears witness to these events and on Yom Ha'Shoah as well as other occasions, she stands up before hundreds of people and, in a strong and rousing voice, defiantly sings in Yiddish, "Zog Nit Keynmol" ("Never say this is the end of the road"), the hymn of the Jewish Partisans.

I was now wide awake. Her brightly painted pink nails symbolized for me the triumph of normality over affliction. On this Shavuot night, these ten pink fingernails seemed to represent the Jewish people's response to centuries of persecution.

As we approached midnight, together with Jewish communities all over the world, we celebrated, in a bond of the generations, Moses receiving the Torah on Mount Sinai and the revelation of The Ten Commandments with a beautiful cantorial melody.

At the same time, those ten pink fingernails seemed to stand as a symbol of Jewish survival, of the incredible will to live and to shout out in defiance for the world to hear, *Look, after everything that's happened, we are still here, living a normal life as Jews in Jewish community. Shalom Aleichem. Peace Be With You.*

Note: Mira Shelub's amazing story is told in her book, "Never the Last Road." A Partisan's Life. Co-authored with Fred Rosenbaum.

Real Citizens

It was June 20, 2012. I sat on the edge of my seat, muscles tensed and ready to spring into action among the forest of rising smiling figures.

As the roll call continued and we alphabetically moved around the world, many of the countries brought to mind a stream of delightful remembered adventures in Belarus, Canada and China. The list continued with people constantly rising.

To my left, "Hong Kong" rose briskly, suited and serious, followed by a more casual "India" to my right. Anan grinned at me as he slowly stood up. Though we had only met thirty minutes previously in the elegant auditorium of the Paramount Theatre in Oakland, we had bonded immediately, exchanging stories about India and England and reminiscing about our favorite flavorful Indian dishes. We now felt like we had been friends for years.

Japan, Russia, Singapore, and Thailand. The roll call continued and I still remained seated, now in the minority. An acorn among a forest of swaying figures, fluttering small flags instead of leaves. I should have been used to this, waiting until last was a familiar experience for me with a family name beginning with the letter Z. How ironic that now my country of origin was also consigning me to the back of the line.

At last the letter U was about to be called and my knees started to propel me upwards as I heard the word "United," only to fall back into my seat again, The United Arab Republic, was definitely not my country of origin. I was so focused on the upping and downing that I then almost missed what I had been so on edge to hear, "The United Kingdom."

I sprang up, glancing around the beautifully restored art deco hall with its rich mellow colors and distinctive designs and, to my amazement, caught sight of my eldest nephew, Daniel, who had just jumped up and was standing at the back of the auditorium waving a flag. He caught my eye and grinned sheepishly.

What was he doing down here with the new immigrants? He was supposed to be up in the balcony with the other guests, cheering me on with his two sons, Little Daniel, aged eleven and Jacob, nine.

He disappeared in a sea of waving flags and the tumultuous chorus of 1300 voices from one hundred and eleven countries reciting, "The Oath of Allegiance," topped by a crescendo of cheers.

As I emerged from the excitement and noise of the auditorium into the main foyer, I was met by three beaming faces.

"Congratulations Vivvy! You're now an American citizen like us," Little Daniel and Jacob shouted, looking at the Certificate of Naturalization I was clutching tightly in my hand. After all, it had taken me twenty-one years to get it.

I laughed, at the same time looking quizzically at Daniel.

"What was that about? Why were you down in the auditorium? You were supposed to be cheering me on from the balcony, not participating in the ceremony."

Daniel looked embarrassed. "Oh, we were late and the balcony was full, so they slipped us in at the back of the auditorium."

"And then what?" I persevered.

Daniel hesitated and then in a rush explained, "You know that when we came to America I was only eight years old and so I became a citizen automatically when mom became one and I always felt something was missing, some defining ceremony. So today, when I found myself in the auditorium, I decided to stand when they called "The United Kingdom," and go through the ceremony with you. It was so special and now at last I feel like a real citizen, just like you. Isn't that great?"

Looking at the happy handsome face of my thirty-five-year-old nephew, I remembered the golden-haired little boy who had arrived here from London to a completely new way of life first in Monterey and then in San Francisco and I suddenly understood his need to actually formalize the process in this citizenship ceremony.

I gave him a big hug and asked, "Well, fellow citizens, what are we going to do to celebrate my new status?"

Quick as a flash, Little Daniel and Jacob replied, "Pizza, ice cream and a walk on the beach at Pedro Point. Come on. Let's go."

Acknowledgments

Thanks....

To my dear parents Ivy and Monty Zielin who brought me up in a loving Jewish family environment, and gave me the confidence to go forth in the world.

To Barbara Rose Brooker, my teacher, muse and friend, who inspired me to write again with her creativity and encouragement.

To Cathy Fiorello, Francee Covington, Michael Gordon, Norma Kauffman, Marsha Michaels and Sue Wood, members of my writer's workshop at the Osher Lifelong Learning Institute at SFSU, who always had my back and brought new perspectives to my writing.

To my sister Avril for her love, friendship and support, and to my environmentally friendly late brother-in-law Bob Brodey, without whom I would not be living here in the United States.

To my nephews, Daniel, Thomas, Little Daniel and Jacob for good times had, memories made and for keeping me on my toes.

To my lovely Gramps Isaac Jacobs, who enjoyed working as a tailor till the age of ninety and taught me early on, that the best way to stay young is to think young.

To my friend Vibhuti Patel, who opened my eyes to the delights of traveling and exploring the world.

To my great fellow adventurers: Jon Spector, Martin Hughes and Abe Shamash.

To Robert Frigo, my partner in The China Ware House Company, who helped me make my dream of building a giftware business from scratch, a reality.

To Maddy Gozman, Gill Mimran and Jennifer Galeria, who have showed me the joys of lifelong friendships, and to all my other wonderful friends and family who have touched my heart in many different parts of the world.

To my family in Israel for their always welcoming smiles and hospitality, and to my cousin Hadassah Mizrachi for her amazing bravery and resilience.

To Keran Davison, for her proofreading, and Mel Margolis for his invaluable help with graphics and design.

To Andy Titcomb of Andy Titcomb Ceramics for his artistry in designing original and quirky teapots.

Last but not least to Henry Slamovich, Mira Shelub, Samuel Sonnenblick and Cantor Henry Drejer for vividly illustrating how, the human spirit can survive and rise above the most painful and destructive of experiences, and soar high to attain life's dreams.

www.ingramcontent.com/pod-product-compliance
Lightning Source LLC
Chambersburg PA
CBHW070053080526
44586CB00013B/1037